Unity between Horse and Rider

Many riders and horse owners are looking for a kinder, more ethical way of interacting with their horses, to fulfil the requirements of the modern Social Licence to Operate but also to enhance their relationship with their animal. In this book, author and expert rider Anne Wilson demonstrates that we need look no further than the teachings of the great classical riding masters, past and present.

Classical teachings are often misunderstood today. This in-depth book on classical principles aims to rectify that, enlightening the reader on techniques which will enhance their own enjoyment as well as that of their horses. Wilson provides a wealth of 'how-to' information, via down-to-earth language and detailed imagery, which will enable readers to put the principles into effect. She throws light on hitherto much misunderstood aspects of horse training, showing that when these principles are employed correctly, the rider or trainer will experience an incomparable feeling of being at one with their horse. Perhaps most importantly, this book will help your horse enjoy 'dancing' with his or her rider, enhancing their physical and mental well-being, as well as their likely longevity.

Unity between Horse and Rider: Classical Training for the Benefit of Both will be of great benefit to riders in any discipline who have basic knowledge and skills but wish to learn a more ethical, fulfilling way of training and riding. For riders, riding professionals, students and trainers, classical riding is the key to a happy life for horse and human alike.

Unity between Horse and Rider

Classical Training for the Benefit of Both

ANNE WILSON

CRC Press
Taylor & Francis Group
Boca Raton London New York

CRC Press is an imprint of the
Taylor & Francis Group, an **informa** business

Front cover image: Photo by Lesley Skipper

First edition published 2025
by CRC Press
2385 NW Executive Center Drive, Suite 320, Boca Raton FL 33431

and by CRC Press
4 Park Square, Milton Park, Abingdon, Oxon, OX14 4RN

CRC Press is an imprint of Taylor & Francis Group, LLC

ISBN: 978-1-032-82195-5 (hbk)
ISBN: 978-1-032-79081-7 (pbk)
ISBN: 978-1-003-50342-2 (ebk)

DOI: 10.1201/9781003503422

Typeset in Dante and Avenir
by Apex CoVantage, LLC

Contents

About the author

Photo Credits: **Anne with PRE Mare Mill Sigilosa, Stable Name Secret**
Photo by Emma Green.

Anne Wilson has been involved with horses all her life and trained with Sylvia Loch. She joined the Classical Riding Club (run by Sylvia Loch) in 1995 and for many years was Regional Liaison Member on behalf of the Club. In 1998, she was awarded the CRC Gold Award Certificate. Anne began writing articles for the CRC Club magazine in 1995. Since then, she has been writing regularly for various equestrian magazines. From 2008 until 2020, she wrote articles every month in Equi-Ads magazine, which was a national publication with around 300,000 circulation. In 2004, her first book, *Top Horse Training Methods Explored*, was published; it became an equestrian best-seller and was pronounced 'Book of the Month' in that year by the British Horse Society. In 2009, her second book, *Riding Revelations – Classical Training from the Beginning*, was published. In 2008, Anne began publishing a quarterly equestrian subscription magazine, in partnership with Susan McBane and Lesley Skipper, titled *Tracking-up*. This is still active today, and she continues to write articles in this publication and is actively involved in its production. This magazine does not carry advertising and is run on a non-profit-making, voluntary basis, for the benefit of horses. To subscribe to *Tracking-up*, email Anne at annewilsondressage@hotmail.co.uk. Alongside her writing career, Anne has been teaching the art of classical riding to individual pupils since around 1995.

Acknowledgements and dedications

I would like to dedicate this book to my wonderful friend and colleague, Lesley Skipper, who tragically passed away in December 2023. She was one of the best friends I ever had. She will remain in my heart forever. Without her, there is no doubt this book would not exist. She took most of the photographs and was a constant inspiration and help to me. She was not only an extremely talented and knowledgeable horse person, but I have never come across a more generous and kind spirit. I thank her husband, Brian, who gave his permission for the reproduction of many of the illustrations.

I would also like a dedication to my wonderful horse, Secret – a Spanish PRE mare, registered name 'Mill Sigilosa'. Most of my sentiments about Lesley apply to Secret: the kindest and most generous horse I have ever known.

Alice Oven of Taylor & Francis has been very supportive and encouraging, and I thank her and the production team, particularly the help from my excellent Project Manager Balaji Karuppanan.

My thanks go to my great friend and mentor, Sylvia Loch, without whom I would never have met Lesley nor acquired the knowledge to write this book. I cannot thank her enough for what she has done for me (and others like me) over the years. Also, for her help with photos for the book. All Sylvia's books and DVDs are available direct from her at SYLVIA LOCH, Long Meadow, Tilbury Juxta Clare, Sudbury, CO9 4JT.

My other great friend, Susan McBane, has been a constant inspiration to me for years now, and without her encouragement I would probably not have written the book.

Kathleen Goulden has been my best friend for sixty years now (how time flies). Although she is not a horse person, her support and encouragement has been great. She has also taken two of the photos in the book.

Last, but definitely not least, I thank my dear partner, David Green, who has put up with me spending so many hours at the computer. He has also been an invaluable help on IT matters and acted as a 'sounding board' for some of my writing.

Many other people have encouraged me, such as my friend Rita Ling, and my thanks go to you all. Without all these people, it is difficult to see that I would have come this far. I thank you all from the bottom of my heart; as well as all the horses of course.

ANNE WILSON – 2025

Introduction

Classical riding and training principles have been used for thousands of years. The benefits have been proven beyond doubt many times over.

However, in these fast-changing times, the art of classical riding has been altered, or defaced, by 'modern' or 'competitive' dressage, resulting in the early breakdown and deaths of many wonderful horses. This may sound like an over-dramatization, but truly it is not.

Dressage is, or should be, the basis of all horse training, no matter which discipline is the chosen path for a particular horse and rider. So, the offending practices which have such a bad effect on horses apply to all disciplines.

The main causes for this sad state of affairs appear to be time, money, fame and ego. It takes many years to correctly train and strengthen a dressage horse, jumper, cross-country horse or any other. When time is not taken for this process, together with the beneficial classical exercises, then the result is the early breakdown and/or death of many, as mentioned earlier. Quite apart from this wastage is the mental unhappiness and stress which so many have to undergo. This actually includes the riders as well as horses!

Fortunately, there are still conscientious, good traditional horse people, breeding, producing or training horses using sound, time-honoured methods, giving horses time to mature before bringing them into work and not rushing their training. These people often work in obscurity and may not call themselves classical, but they actually use most of the same methods. They may not make so much money and may not be acclaimed for their brilliant work, but they have a happy and fulfilled relationship with their horses, content in the knowledge that their art has not been compromised for the sake of fame or fortune.

DOI: 10.1201/9781003503422-1

Figure 0.1 Secret and Anne Having Fun
Photo by Kathleen Goulden.

I believe that there is a change afoot in the grass roots of riding today. Many people are searching for a kinder, more ethical way of interacting with their horses, and it is possible that they have not yet found the wondrous experience of dancing with their horse, which the true classical art can bring about. It is beneficial for mental and physical health, for both horse and rider. There is no more natural nor ethical way to train and ride, as classical techniques work with nature to strengthen, enhance the horse's natural gaits, and improve the human body's strength and poise, protecting the precious equine and human spines – working with the laws of nature such as gravity and staying in equilibrium with the horse's centre of balance. Eventually, the aids given by the rider are miniscule and not noticeable to the onlooker. In true classical dressage, it is as though horse and rider are moving as one – one body blending into the other. I am absolutely sure that this is as fulfilling and pleasurable to the horse as it is to the rider. This can be seen by the happy, confident expression in the horse's eye and the relaxed, freely swinging tail.

All this comes with an uplifting experience for both partners, from which true unity is achieved and a deep love can grow.

I hope that this book can help to show the way to enlightenment for many grass-roots riders.

Note: Throughout this book, the words 'he' or 'his' in reference to the horse include the female 'her' or 'hers'.

Classical riding for everyone

1

The term *classical* riding is often much misunderstood. Firstly, many people think of it as elitist or consisting of advanced or difficult dressage. The word *classical* actually means that it has its origins in past centuries and has passed the test of time. Although there are slight differences of opinion in the classical world, its principles have, and always will, remain the same to any true classicist. This is because it is based on the laws of nature, such as gravity, and the natural biomechanics of the horse. Although horses are bred differently for different purposes, their basic make-up and way of movement has remained the same for thousands of years.

The word dressage means to 'dress' or prepare the horse for whatever work it is intended, and all dressage has its origins in classical horsemanship. Therefore, all horses, from big Warmbloods down to Shetland ponies, should be prepared for their work by basic dressage.

Whatever you intend to do with your horse, he will benefit from basic classical dressage, and classical merely means 'correct' in this sense.

Rollkur or hyperflexion of the head and neck

In the 1990s, I, along with many others in the Classical Riding Club (at the behest of Sylvia Loch, the Club's founder), organised petitions, gaining hundreds of signatures, in an attempt to outlaw draw-reins. These reins are an easy way for riders to force the head in towards the chest, by sheer mechanical force. Sylvia has been untiring in her quest to educate the world to the benefits and necessity of classical principles.

DOI: 10.1201/9781003503422-2

Figure 1.1 Rollkur

Here we see the horse's head and neck pulled inwards, with nose towards the chest, and the neck and back of the horse in tension – not a happy sight. Photo by Lesley Skipper.

In February 2008, Susan McBane and I (the entire *Tracking-up* Magazine team in the UK at that time) composed a letter to the Fédération Equestre Internationale (FEI, the worldwide governing body of equestrian sport) imploring them to outlaw the practice of rollkur (extreme hyperflexion of the head and neck). We gained the signatures of a number of top horse people worldwide and published this letter, along with the reply from the FEI, in the very first issue of *Tracking-up*. I don't think we were the only ones making overtures of this kind to the FEI because shortly afterwards, they issued a statement saying that they were against the practice and that it would not be allowed in practice arenas and other places. However, as we all know, this ruling has not been strictly adhered to and is still quite common today. The issue seems to have been further complicated by the FEI allowing a certain amount of low, deep and round (LDR), which perhaps, in the right hands, should be different from rollkur but in most instances is just rollkur by another name. In my opinion, it should be outlawed.

Followers of classical equestrian principles all over the world have been trying to improve the lot of the horse for a long time now, and it is very sad that the issue still has not gone away. This applies to all disciplines.

Rollkur is just one of the aspects of cruel, damaging, so-called schooling practices.

The German vet Dr. Gerd Heuschmann's brilliant and brave book *Tug of War – Classical Versus 'Modern' Dressage* was published by J.A. Allen in 2006 (Ref: 1.1), showing all the scientific, veterinary reasons why this type of practice is so bad for the horse. I applaud his, and his publisher's, bravery in speaking out for the sake of the horse then, and I do the same now with the book *Broken or Beautiful – The Struggle of Modern Dressage* by Dominique Barbiere and Liz Conrod, published by Xenophon Press in 2021 (Ref: 1.2).

Other aspects of bad riding/training

The authors of *Broken or Beautiful* have read all the FEI rules right back to 1958, and there have been many versions since then, so that must have been a mammoth task!

The authors point out that the first Olympic Games featuring dressage, in 1921, were intended to bring together the French and German schools and to produce universal classical principles. The first Olympic Games was strictly amateur. No money was involved; it was strictly forbidden. Dominique Barbiere tells us it was a friendly sharing of helpful ideas, always with the horse's best interests at the forefront. It was then that the FEI was formed "for the express purpose of protecting the welfare of horses now participating in equestrian games. They did this by using prescribed rules for competitors used as guidelines. The Classical Principles are the foundation for these rules" (Ref: 1.2).

FEI rules are based on classical principles

The FEI rule book is based upon the principles set down by Francois Robichon de la Guérinière (back in the 1700s), one of the most revered classical masters. If all these rules were adhered to, then all competitive dressage would be classical. Unfortunately, some judges have deviated from their own rule book and reward some bad practices.

We should recognise and praise the good judges

Of course, there are good judges who understand and abide by the FEI rule book and remain staunchly classical, but some 'modern' riders criticise these judges and actually try to avoid competing under their judgement.

Many good judges who believe in classical principles must feel somewhat the same as I do; however, it must be extremely difficult for them to speak out.

Although I appear to criticise a lot of 'modern' riders; I cannot actually blame them for what they believe since they are relying on everything they have learnt from their instructors, some of whom may well be successful competitors and are therefore deemed to be correct. Some competition riders are still very classical, but unfortunately, they are in the minority, and many of the role models for young riders are not classical.

It is an eye opener to me that the 'powers that be' have even changed some of the rules to accommodate the inadequacies of modern training.

An example of this is concerning the shoulder-in.

In the 1963 version of the FEI rules (Ref: 1.3), the shoulder-in was described as "a movement to be done at 45 degrees with crossing of the legs". This is clearly the original shoulder-in as invented by Francois Robichon de la Guérinière (on whose teachings I have always believed the FEI rule book is largely based).

In the 1971 version of the rules, the 45-degree angle of the shoulder-in was changed to a 30-degree angle, which is obviously the three-track shoulder-in we see today.

I have nothing at all against the three-track shoulder-in during training, but it is a stepping-stone towards the greater angle of the four track. The 30-degree angle is much less demanding, and it is not the way in which Guérinière intended the shoulder-in to be ridden.

It was in fact the Duke of Newcastle who first devised the shoulder-in, but it was Guérinière who refined it, and much more benefit was gained by following his methods.

The piaffe

Another example of a change of the rule book to accommodate faulty training concerns the piaffe. Originally, the piaffe was described and taught by the masters as basically being a trot on the spot with lightness and extreme collection.

I quote from Guérinière's book *School of Horsemanship* (Ref: 1.3):

> To Piaffe; this is the action the horse makes when it passages on the spot.

Figure 1.2 The White Stallions of Vienna
The granidiere of the Spanish Riding School; the world renowned epitome of classical riding. This also shows the humility of the riders. – 'Image courtesy of Alamy.com'.

I now quote from *Broken or Beautiful* (Ref: 1.4):

> The ultimate air of the Grand Prix test is the piaffer. In the newest version of FEI rules Piaffer is not only no longer called a trot, it is no longer required to be on the spot. The entire definition of Piaffer is changed. Quite frankly, this is because the top riders in the world can no longer do it!

Fortunately, most of the FEI rules remain as laid down by Guérinière and are therefore based on sound classical principles; if only they were all adhered to!

The reason that modern training techniques cannot come up to Guérinière's standard is because not enough time is taken to prepare the horse according to classical principles, that is, strengthening the hindquarters, joints and tendons gradually so that the horse can happily take weight back onto the haunches in order to collect correctly. When this time-honoured (and time-consuming) practice is not adhered to, training descends into a 'compression' of the horse instead of true collection on a light rein. Then, of course, the horse is unable to perform the piaffe correctly. As well as this, the horse is unable to perform many other movements with flexibility, fluidity, grace and joy, as he should.

The purpose of dressage

Dressage is designed to physically and mentally prepare the horse to carry the rider with the optimum amount of ease in the best-balanced way. All the exercises are designed to build up strength and flexibility in the back, joints and tendons, especially strengthening the hind legs, so that the horse can take more weight on the hindquarters, relieving the front legs of the extra pressure which they necessarily are burdened with once a rider is aboard. All these exercises need to be done carefully, and strength must be built up slowly so that the horse comes to a naturally more 'round' frame, which emanates from strength in the hindquarters, hence the phrase 'the horse should be ridden from back to front' – never pulled into an outline from the front.

Horses naturally carry more weight on the forehand, but when the weight of the rider is added, this causes undue strain on the forelegs and is one of the main causes of arthritis and tendon breakdown as the horse ages. A horse carefully prepared in the classical way has a much healthier and longer life expectancy than his counterparts who have been allowed to slop along on the forehand for most of their lives. Also, those who have been brought on too quickly, at an early age, or pulled in from the front end into rollkur, or hyperflexion, very often suffer physical breakdown at an early age.

For all disciplines

Whatever your chosen discipline, a basic grounding in classical dressage will greatly benefit your horse. Added to this, he will be a much more pleasant ride; he will be lighter in the forehand, easier to turn, more agile and a safer ride. Riding with an independent classical seat is much safer and better balanced than riding with a 'chair' seat, as is frequently seen.

A chair seat is when the rider's seat is at the back of the saddle with the legs too far forward, putting too much weight on the weakest part of the horse's back and making the rider most unstable and likely to go 'out the side door' at the slightest spook.

The classical seat is not just for dressage. It can easily be adapted for jumping and cross country by shortening the stirrups a little, making it easier for the rider to follow the centre of gravity forward by folding from the hips and lifting the seat slightly off the saddle. All the other laws of gravity remain the same. The weight aids for turning and re-aligning the horse before a jump render the horse better balanced and more

Figure 1.3 A Young Classical Rider

Note the upright position and sympathetic contact with the horse's mouth. Photo of Alexa on Ike. Photo courtesy of Photos by Alex.

manoeuvrable, so the rider does not need to rely on hauling on the reins as is often the case.

If you are a happy hacker, you will find classical training a real boon to your enjoyment. Your horse will be lighter and easier to turn, and you will feel much more in control without any harsh aids. Your horse will be better at negotiating turns and uneven ground, and he will be more likely to stay sound and live longer if he is capable of taking some of the weight onto the haunches. Your seat will be deeper in the saddle, and both you and your horse will be safer.

Weight aids from the beginning

It is a source of sadness to me that the simple weight aids are not very often taught to new riders at riding schools these days. They are simple for the

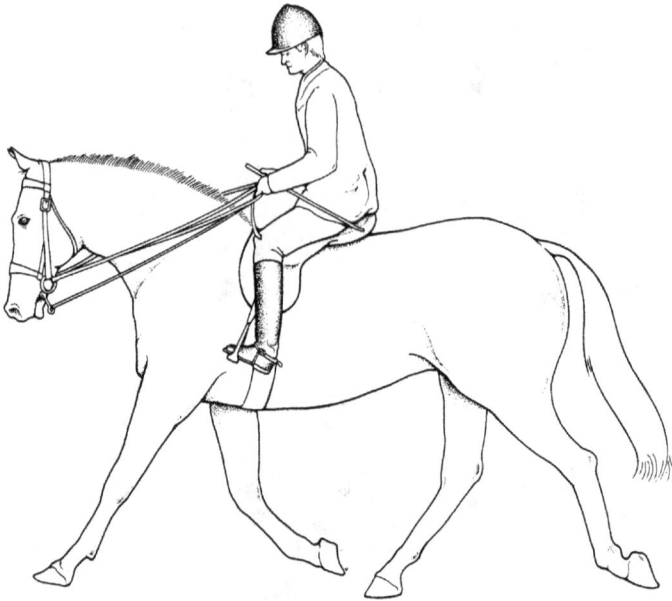

Figure 1.4 Chair Seat

The stirrups are too short for flat work, forcing the seat to the back of the saddle (the weakest point of the horse's back), and the upper body is collapsed forward, putting the rider in front of the centre of balance, ready to fall 'out the side door' at the first trip or spook of the horse. Figure courtesy of Lesley Skipper.

rider and a natural thing for the horse to respond to, and they are much more comfortable.

For instance, to turn left, the rider should put a little weight on the left stirrup, turn the head and shoulders to the left, give a gentle feel on the left rein, draw the outside (right) leg very slightly back, and hold the right rein in position to support the horse's right shoulder. In this way the horse can make a very balanced left turn, following the weight and position of the rider, without falling onto the left shoulder and being pulled in the mouth with an over-exaggerated left head and neck flexion.

The rider's weight transference should be fairly miniscule. This will be felt by the horse, and it is a natural reaction for the horse to follow this weight transference. They don't have to be taught; it is done automatically. If you were carrying a horizontal pole above your head, the easiest way to carry it would be in the middle with equal weight either side. If one side starts to feel heavier, your reaction will be to move in that direction, so you stay under the centre of gravity.

Figure 1.5 An Excellent Classical Jumping Position

An excellent classical jumping position – Peter Robeson OBE, (a top Olympic show jumper of the 1960's, sadly no longer with us). Note the rider's upper body folded forward with seat above the hips, legs down and hands following the movement of the horse either side of the neck, giving the horse room to stretch. – Image courtesy of Alamy.com.

The longevity of the horse

When trained classically, the horse can look forward to a long and healthy life. Often this lifespan can be decades longer than that of his non-classically trained counterparts.

The classical movements are all designed to build strength and flexibility of the joints, tendons, ligaments and back – in fact all parts of the horse. The main thing is that nothing is rushed. Joints are not damaged by over-work too soon, but strength is gradually built up, over years rather than months. In this way, limbs are strengthened rather than damaged. The pay-back for this patience on behalf of the trainer is that the onset of arthritis and tendon breakdown is much less likely.

When the horse has been trained and strengthened through the correct exercises, he is able to lift his forehand and carry more weight on his back legs and quarters. The physiology of the back legs is much more able to carry this weight, and thus, the front legs are, to a significant degree, relieved of this burden. The weight is, of course, much more significant whilst carrying a rider.

All of this, combined with general caring and careful management of the horse's lifestyle, means that the horse can live a happy, active and long life.

The classical ethos

The ethos of all classical riders has been laid down by the great classical masters throughout the centuries. The first written word on the subject was around 400 BC, when Xenophon wrote his book *The Art of Horsemanship*, published latterly in 1962 by J.A. Allen (Ref: 1.5). In this book, Xenophon describes, amongst many other things, the best place for a rider to sit on the horse's back to give the horse optimum comfort and the chance to carry his rider in the best possible way. The strongest part of the horse's back is just behind the withers, around the fourteenth vertebrae. This is where the ribs are at their longest and therefore the strongest part of the horse's back.

The rider should sit tall and erect, without slouching, with the weight of the legs falling gently down towards the heels. This has been proven throughout the centuries since then to be the most beneficial position for both horse and rider. Everything that Xenophon describes is with the horse's best interests in mind, and this is the ethos of classical riding. The ethos does not stop at riding. Everything we do with our horses should be considerate and kind. If it is not, then we cannot call ourselves classical horsemen. This is not to say that the horse should not have discipline. Horses thrive on good discipline, but it must be fair and kind.

Everything is based on mutual respect with a view to the best long-term interests of the horse. Anything other than this is not true classicism but merely a travesty of the word.

Classicism also educates the rider in a broader sense, making him more aware of the needs and feelings of others, teaching him patience, perseverance and humility, all of which can be carried forward into general life.

Since Xenophon, there have been many more great classical masters. There are modern masters alive today whose talent and wisdom are breathtaking. Throughout all these years (although there have been, and still are, some minor disagreements), the main principles and ethos remain the same. The masters are unanimous in the belief that classical riding is the best way for the horse to live a full, happy and long life.

A word of warning

Whilst there are many good classical trainers around today, there are always some who 'get on the bandwagon'. They call themselves classical when they are not. The best way of sorting out the charlatans from the real thing is to remember that if they ask a pupil to do anything which is forceful or harsh, then that is not classical.

On the other side of the coin, there are many excellent trainers who do not call themselves classical. Just because they do not use the word 'classical' does not mean that they are not using classical principles, sometimes even without knowing it.

The website of the Classical Riding Club (www.classicalriding.co.uk), founded and run by Sylvia Loch, has a Trainers Directory that provides details of registered trainers in various regions. Although these trainers are not actually vetted, they do sign a declaration that they adhere to classical principles, and I think it much more likely that you will find a suitable classical teacher from this source rather than a random search. Also, you may learn much merely by joining the online club (there is no charge). You can follow the questions and answers and may wish to contribute to the conversations.

Recommendations by word of mouth may be a good source of finding a good instructor, but then you must consider whether the person who has given the recommendation really understands the difference between classical and modern riding.

A general search on the Internet may well find what you are looking for, but bear in mind that choosing a riding instructor is a mine field, and one has to be very discerning; ask a lot of pertinent (but not impertinent) questions before making a booking. Even then, one cannot be one hundred per cent sure that the trainer/instructor is actually what they purport to be. Many instructors say they teach classically when in fact they have little or no idea of classical teachings. If you are after a good classical teacher, and I hope you are, it's a good idea not only to ask about the person's background and training but also to enquire as to which of the classical masters they most admire. Many people claim to have trained with this or that famous trainer when in fact they only had one lesson, or maybe they just worked on the yard as a groom. However, the question of which masters they admire or have studied will usually put a charlatan on the back foot as they will have limited knowledge in this field, whereas a true classicist will probably bubble over with enthusiasm about, for instance, Guérinière, Egon Von Neindorf, Podhajsky or a later classical master such as Sylvia Loch.

It will be immensely helpful, during these initial enquiries, if you have familiarised yourself with some of the basic principles of classical equitation. You can do this by reading books by well-respected classical trainers, such as those just mentioned. The more reading you can do, the better. Some of what you read may seem hard to understand at first (that is one of the things you want your new instructor to help you with). Remember that if you read slightly conflicting instruction, there are always going to be areas of disagreement between trainers, but these areas should be minor. Each trainer will have a slightly different approach; however, the basic foundation of classicism should be consistent. If you read enough, you will find that there is a solid foundation of principles running through each of the masters' books. In this way you should be in a much better position to judge whether your prospective instructor is genuinely, and knowledgeably, classical.

Of course, I hope that reading this book will give you much insight into the world of classicism.

References

Ref: 1.1 – 'Tug of War: Classical Versus "Modern" Dressage' – Heuschmann, Dr. Gerd – Translated by Abelshauser Reina – J.A. Allen – 2007.

Ref: 1.2 – 'Broken or Beautiful – The Struggle of Modern Dressage' – Barbier, Dominique & Conrod, Liz – Xenophon Press – 2021.

Ref: 1.3 – 'Federation Equestre Internationale Rule Book' – FEI – 1963.

Ref: 1.4 – 'School of Horsemanship' – de la Guérinière, Francois Robichon – Translated by Tracy Boucher – J.A. Allen – 2003.

Ref: 1.5 – 'The Art of Horsemanship' – Xenophon – J.A. Allen – 1962.

What is going wrong today? **2**

Too much too young

In my opinion, a lot of the problems today are caused by the training of horses being rushed to an extreme degree. This begins with the breeders who are seeking a quick turnover and want to show that their young horses have reached a high level of achievement, therefore they will command a higher price. This has gone on for many years now, but there seem to be more of the buying public who are unaware of the dangers of this practice and who 'buy into' the culture of 'look what he can do at the age of three'. Some people, very mistakenly, think this is good!

All good horsemen know that a horse is still a baby at three years of age and should not even be backed; or if he is, it should be merely a quick sit upon and no more.

The racing industry

The fact that all flat racehorses are started when they should still be with their dams does nothing to dispel the idea that this is okay. Flat horse racing begins when the horse is termed 'a two-year-old', but because of the Thoroughbred stud book registration system in the UK being such that all horses born in a specific year are officially born on 1st January of that year, many of the horses running as two-year-olds are actually a lot younger than that. This has been going on for generations now and has become accepted.

DOI: 10.1201/9781003503422-3

But should it be? Most racehorses' careers are finished before they are even properly mature, and the vast majority are dead before they even reach their teens, at which age a classically trained horse would be considered to be in its prime.

The situation with point to point and hurdlers is a little different in that they do not race quite so early, but their life expectation is still not good, and they are still started too early.

It is a fact that horses do not mature until, at the earliest, around seven years old, and some breeds, particularly large ones, mature very much later than this, possibly eight or nine. When I say 'mature', I mean that their bone structure is still growing. This does not mean that they should not be ridden at all, but the proper work should not be started until around the age of five, and even then, they should be considered as very young, and great care should be taken not to over-strain their joints. No matter what age it is begun, work should be slow, careful and graduated, taking into account the horse's fitness and stage of growth.

Succession planning

One possible solution to the worrying problem of horses working when they're too young is for owners to consider adopting a succession planning approach whereby horses are allowed to develop at a natural rate. This could be achieved by the acquisition of differing ages of horses to ensure that there are always horses of a suitable age to come into work.

This policy is often adopted by commercial companies where a large number of human employees is involved.

Horses used in war in the past

I suppose it is common practice to start horses early as this has been happening for many years now. During the first world war and before, many horses were needed to go to the battle field, and no one had time to honour the riding masters' pleas for patience. Horses were expendable items, but that is certainly no reason to treat them as such today. My belief is that many people who buy a young horse from, say, a dealer who boasts that he has won this or that in jumping competitions, as well as hunted and done well in three-day-events, really believe that this is a good thing and are just in blissful ignorance of the damage which has already been done to their prospective partner.

The innocent buyer

I had one very nice, kind, and patient lady who came to me for lessons on a gorgeous Irish-bred horse of around 16.2 hands (hh). She bought him as a five-year-old from Ireland and proceeded to gently hack him around the village. She came to me for lessons so she could benefit herself and her horse by learning the classical weight aids etc., and to help the horse take weight back onto the haunches and so preserve his front legs to hopefully give him a good, long life. Unfortunately, the poor horse had been hunted, jumped and done just about everything in Ireland before he came to her. He periodically had problems in his back, hocks, hips and elsewhere. She spent a fortune on osteopaths, vets, new saddles and so on. Sadly, after three years, the vet declared him unfit to ride. He had advanced arthritis at the age of eight. This horse is very fortunate; he has been turned out in the field with a field shelter and is living a happy life in retirement with another horse which she has purchased to ride. This one has very little 'miles on the clock', so she should be okay this time. Her damaged horse will be well cared for the rest of his life, but the same cannot be said for most horses in this situation. It is a crying shame that such a lovely horse has to be retired when he is hardly mature, and all for the sake of time and money.

Longevity of the famous white stallions of Vienna

At the Spanish Riding School of Vienna, the famous Lipizzaner stallions are not backed until they are four or five years old, and they spend around eight years in training before they are anywhere near ready to be shown in a performance. Their training is slow but sure. They are only ridden for about half an hour per day in their early years. They gradually build up their strength and suppleness, and each horse is treated as an individual, that is, some will need more time on a particular exercise than others, or may not be ready at the same age as others for a particular exercise. In this way, their longevity is great; they often travel the world and perform well into their late twenties or even early thirties. A favourite saying at the Spanish Riding School is 'make haste slowly'. The Lipizzan is a long-lived breed, but this would not be possible without the classical training and ethos to which they bear witness.

The competition scene

Similar problems arise in the competition world, and all disciplines are subject to this form of cruelty. The breeders want to sell their horses for as high a price as they can, and the owners, trainers and sponsors want the most out of their horses (as they see it, their investments) as soon as possible.

Some judges have bought into this circle of greed and desire for fame and fortune, many of whom (I have been told) are afraid not to give high marks to certain well-connected competitors for fear of not being asked to judge again. Thus, the FEI rules have largely been thrown out of the window. Thankfully, this is not the case regarding all judges, so there is hope that we can regain some good principles in training.

As well as being started too young, most competition horses are badly trained by such methods as rollkur (extreme hyperflexion of the head and neck, as described in Chapter 1). This causes undue stress and often permanent damage to the horse. Because this is so widespread in the competition scene, it has become commonplace in grass roots riding to try to 'make the horse round' by pulling the head and neck inwards. This may not be complete rollkur, but it is very detrimental. You cannot make a horse 'round' from the front. The round appearance can only properly come by the correct build-up exercises to teach and enable the horse to take more weight onto the haunches. It cannot be forced; it comes naturally when the horse is ready mentally and physically. By pulling the horse's head inwards, all that is achieved is an unhappy, uncomfortable horse with a stiff back whose hind legs cannot come underneath his body properly and are generally left trailing behind.

To rectify this effect of hind legs trailing, some unscrupulous trainers have devised all manner of contraptions to lunge the horse, with reins and ropes pulling him this way and that. Needless to say, this just compounds the problem, and the horse becomes stiffer and more damaged.

There are no kind or effective short cuts to true horsemanship. Just watch a performance of the Spanish Riding School, and you can easily see the joy of fluid, supple movement, carried out in a calm, gentle way. This is true art in movement.

The false collection

The practice of rollkur, or otherwise pulling the horse in from the front end whilst driving it forward with the legs in an attempt to make it appear to have a 'round outline', is actually seeking a false collection. This is not actually collection at all – it is compression, and so many horses on the competition scene particularly, in all disciplines, are compressed like this today.

As I keep reiterating, true collection can only come from strength behind, built up over time.

Figure 2.1 Natural Arching of the Neck

You can see the beginnings of self-carriage and natural arching of the neck. Here I am on my horse Secret. In the beginning, this self-carriage can only be achieved for a few seconds at a time, but it can be built-up over time, as the horse becomes stronger. Photo by Lesley Skipper.

Just as bad as hyperflexion of the head and neck is the practice of pulling the horse's head upwards and nose inwards in an attempt to create an arched neck. This, again, causes compression of the whole frame of the horse and causes damage. The arching of the neck will also come naturally, when the horse's back and muscles are strong enough, and he will arch his neck without any assistance from the trainer.

The proof that something is going wrong today is in the fact that, as reported in Europe, nearly sixty per cent of insured horses are dead before they are eight years old! This surely speaks for itself!

The problems in riding schools

In my younger days, many riding schools were run by ex-military personnel and organised on a very strict regime. Although it may have been a fairly harsh environment for new riders, mostly I believe the horses were well cared for. Pupils were taught in a way which included an independent seat;

one which encouraged us to acquire 'quiet hands', which were a much sought-after accomplishment in those days. Quiet hands don't seem to be mentioned much nowadays, except by true classical teachers.

At one establishment in the Midlands, UK, I remember that the horses were so fit and full of beans that no one was allowed to go out on a hack until they could jump a three-foot fence with no reins and stirrups – no mean feat; I wouldn't like to do it now. It did teach us how to balance without the help of reins, and you had to sit in a classical position, merely taking your upper body forward as the horse took off, to relieve the horse's back of your weight and to stop the upward thrust on the rider's seat at strike off. Your legs had to be kept down underneath your hips and your centre of balance was over the horse's. Your seat needed to be pushed slightly outward, behind you, just slightly above the saddle. On landing, you had to quickly resume your upright, poised position with your seat back in the saddle. If you didn't do these things, you simply couldn't stay on. At the time, I didn't know this was the classical jumping seat, and this fact was never mentioned. This very harsh way of teaching would never be allowed today because of health and safety issues. We did all suffer a lot of falls, and I'm not sure it was good in many ways, but it taught us the right way to jump, albeit in a dangerous way.

Having said this, I never remember being taught the basic weight aids, which are so important in classical riding. There was a lot missing in our equestrian education, but it was better than what I see and hear of mostly today, such as pupils being told to kick on, pull the left rein to turn left and so on.

I am also told that riding schools are no longer allowed to teach riders on the lunge without stirrups because of health and safety. Also, probably, because of insurance issues. This is such a shame because a steady, experienced, lunge horse can teach a rider so much without stirrups, and it can be reasonably safe if a neck strap is employed for emergency use.

In recent years, many good riding schools have gone out of business due to financial pressures, insurance companies' requirements and so on. I can only think that, unless more good schools are set up, the way ahead for good equestrianism will be through good freelance teaching and books.

The benefit of teaching yourself from books is seriously underrated. It is, doubtless, a distinct advantage to have a knowledgeable person on the ground to instruct you, but it is better to have no one there than to be given the wrong advice. Once you have acquired the basic riding skills, it is quite possible to advance on the classical learning ladder if you not only read but also study in depth the books of the masters, both old and new – providing you choose the right ones. If you find something difficult to understand at first, you may understand it later on, say a year on, if you go back to it. So, reading and re-reading the right books is a must. There are also plenty of DVDs by modern masters which will give you visual instruction of what to aim for.

Never be put off or undermined by criticism from 'modern' riders who have not learned the wisdom of classicism. If you keep your horse on a livery yard, you are likely to have plenty of critical people, some of whom may be successful competitors, who think they know best, but many times, they know nothing. It can be very lonely and isolating to be the only person doing things differently, and you may be the subject of lots of ridicule. Be strong and steadfast; try not to listen to them. You can politely tell them, if asked, that the principles you are following have proved, for more than two thousand years, to be the best possible path to brilliant equestrianism and the best for the horse. However, you may still be laughed at! I know this is very hard to take, so it is best, if possible, not to become deeply involved in conversation with people who think they (or their Grand Prix rider instructors) know best. There are people who cannot be reasoned with and who refuse to consider a different point of view. Try not to be affected by them; join clubs of like-minded people, such as the Classical Riding Club, so that you don't feel quite so much like you're 'swimming against the tide'.

The classical seat

3

A good seat encompasses much more than just the seat-bones; it includes the thighs, legs and torso of the rider.

All the great horse masters throughout the ages (since Xenophon around 400 BC, as mentioned in the previous chapter) have agreed, in principle, upon the basis of the classical seat. How sad that we still see people in a 'chair' seat today, doubtless damaging their own as well as their horses' backs!

A first-class saddle fitter is essential

Of course, a well-fitting saddle is essential for this to be possible. It should sit just behind the withers but be designed in such a way that it does not interfere with the horse's shoulders. This requirement will obviously mean that not all saddle designs will fit every horse since all horses' conformation is different. The most expensive saddle in the world, even if it is the right size (i.e., gullet/width and length) for the horse, could still be totally wrong for some horses and could cause considerable discomfort, pain and/or damage. Although the seat needs to be big enough for the rider, it should not be so long as to put weight onto the weakest part of the back near the loins.

A first-class saddle fitter is essential to fit the saddle to any horse. The size of the seat, to accommodate the rider and help put him in the correct position, is also to be considered. There are no economical short cuts in saddle fitting. It is well worth paying for a well-qualified and experienced saddle fitter. It will pay dividends in the end.

DOI: 10.1201/9781003503422-4

All horses change shape as they mature, as well as during training when their muscles build up. So, the saddle needs to be checked by the fitter on a regular basis. In the early days of training this could be every six months; however, there is good news on this subject – most modern saddles have changeable gullets, meaning that there can be quite a lot of room for adjustment in width and for adjustment in the flocking in other areas. Unless your horse is very young and likely to grow tremendously, then it should be quite possible to buy a saddle which can fit your horse for life, providing, of course, the necessary checks and adjustments are carried out by the fitter on a regular basis.

If your horse is young and likely to grow a lot, then you can always buy a synthetic saddle which is normally a little cheaper. It may be that this saddle will only be suitable for a year or so, at which point you can part exchange it. These can also have adjustable gullets and be otherwise fairly changeable by way of flocking. Alternatively, there is nothing wrong with a second hand saddle, whatever age your horse is. It all depends upon the fit and finding a good saddle fitter.

Bear in mind that your horse should not be ridden much, if at all, before the age of about four or five, depending on his development. But even then, many breeds do not fully mature until about the age of eight, or even older, and can change shape considerably in this time.

A good independent seat

We cannot talk about the seat itself in isolation as it affects, and is affected by, the rest of the rider's body. By 'independent' seat, we mean one which is safe, secure and not reliant on other ways in which to stay there, such as holding onto the reins or gripping with the legs. The seat should be able to stay deep and adhered to the saddle, whilst the legs are used to guide the horse and the upper body stays in good posture, but if the seat is not secure in the first place, this will be impossible.

Most children, when mounting for the first time, will naturally sit in a fairly good position, especially if bareback. This is probably because it is the most comfortable and natural position. For us older people, it may take a little more effort and practise. Unfortunately, our daily lives, often sedentary in front of computers, bending over whilst pushing vacuum cleaners, bending as we muck out stables and push wheelbarrows, all tend to make us slouch. However, good posture is beneficial to our health all of the time, giving our lungs a chance to expand fully and saving our precious backs from injury. When we ride, it is crucially important for other reasons as

Figure 3.1 The Classical Seat

Here I am on my horse Secret, in the sitting phase of the rising trot, therefore, my upper body is very slightly inclined forward ready for the next rise. Photo by Lesley Skipper.

well, such as balance, ability to influence the horse's way of going and, of course, to save the horse's equally precious back.

So, the first thing is to sit up tall with the shoulders back and down. The chest needs to be expanded – this is vital, as is a tummy slightly pushed forwards (but not too much, as later on this is an aid unto itself). Many people find this concept easier if they think of advancing the waist towards the hands, as Sylvia Lock advises in many of her excellent books. The expansion of the chest and the development of toned abdominal and back muscles is something which must be worked upon. Strong core muscles are responsible for keeping the rider upright, in balance and safe.

Figure 3.2 Another Good Example of the Classical Seat
Photo by Lesley Skipper.

By 'strong' and 'toned' muscles, I definitely do not mean tense muscles. Tension in the back and buttock muscles not only will cause impact to both horse and rider but also will cause the rider to bounce up and down unnecessarily. The rider's core needs to be toned and strong enough to hold the rider upright so the rider is in control of their own bodyweight. The buttock and lower back muscles should be toned but soft enough to allow some give and take to absorb the impact of the movement of the horse. This does not mean that the rider should sit up tall and stiff, nor does it mean any exaggeration of movement in the lower back muscles, moving back and forth with the movement unnecessarily. The latter causes pressure pushing back and forth on the saddle.

It takes time for the necessary muscles to be built up by the rider, and lunge lessons are an excellent way of doing this.

The hips and legs

The rider's hips need to be opened as much as possible to allow the legs to drape around the horse, thus facilitating what we call a 'deep seat' – that is, sitting as deep in the saddle as possible rather than bouncing around on top of it. The rider must be wary not to clench the buttocks (as sometimes happens when one is nervous). Apart from making the rider bounce excessively, it is likely to cause the hips and thighs to turn outward, which prevents the all-important opening of the hips. It is most desirable to have flat thighs against the horse, but nature did not make all of us without a degree of excess flesh in this area. Don't despair; these difficulties can be overcome. The rider needs to practise leg exercises, swinging the leg back and forth, without stirrups, and then let the legs hang down. This should give a feeling of allowing the thigh to be closer to the horse, with the fleshy part pushed towards the back of the leg.

The whole of the rider's legs should be allowed to drape around the horse, most of the time lying gently on the horse's sides, until they are needed to give aids. The upper thighs should definitely be thought of as part of the seat.

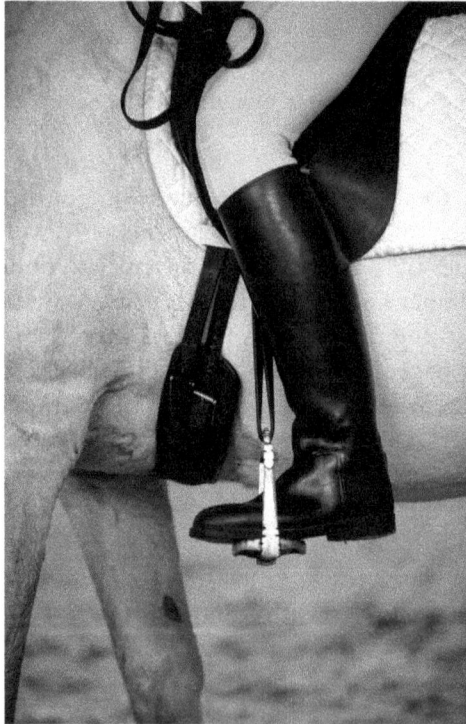

Figure 3.3 A Good 'On the Girth' Leg Position
Note the 'on the girth' position is actually slightly behind the girth, with the heel directly under the hip and the toe roughly aligning with the girth. Photo courtesy of Lesley Skipper.

The knee should be bent slightly, allowing the weight to fall down towards the heel which, when using stirrups, should not be higher than the toe. The toe should ideally be (when not giving an aid) roughly in line with the girth. The ball of the foot should rest on the stirrup with the toe turned slightly outwards. The degree of the outward turn of the toe will depend on the rider's stage of training and/or muscle tone and shape of legs. Ideally, as the rider progresses in training, the toe will turn more towards a front-facing position. This also depends slightly on the shape of the horse's sides. The desirable forward facing toe position follows on from the front part of the rider's inner thigh lying flat against the horse's sides and a generally deep seat. As mentioned before, this cannot happen overnight; it has to be worked on.

Exercises to help

When riding without stirrups, it is perfectly permissible for the toes to be allowed to hang down below the heel, with the leg relaxed, allowing a normal gravitational pull. If the toe is held in a raised position, this causes a certain amount of tension and stiffness, which can transfer up the leg. It is important for the rider to feel that their weight is falling down into their heel, regardless of toe position.

Developing a good seat on the lunge

By far the best way to develop a good seat is on the lunge. Many riders at the Spanish Riding School of Vienna spend years being taught on the lunge on their schoolmaster stallions before they are ever allowed to ride independently.

A good seat needs to be deep and independent. This means, as mentioned previously, that the hips need to be as wide apart as possible. This is only possible when the ligaments in the groin area can be stretched to allow the widening of the hips to the optimum degree. If one has not ridden before, this will take months to achieve. The wider the hips can open, then the deeper the seat can be into the saddle. This will only be effective if the buttock muscles and inner thighs are toned without tension or gripping. Any gripping with these muscles will make the seat come upwards and bounce in the saddle. So, the buttock and upper, inner thigh muscles must absorb the movement. There must also be no gripping with the calf muscles, for the same reason. The toes should be turned as

Figure 3.4 A Rider in the Rising Trot

Here is a very good rider, consolidating his position in the rising trot on the lunge. Photo courtesy of Brian and Lesley Skipper.

much as possible towards the front, with the inside of the knee against the saddle. Again, this will not be possible until the buttocks and upper thighs are supple and toned so that the legs can correctly drape around the horse with the inner thighs lying flat against the horse. This all needs to be worked on.

All of these issues are best addressed when on the lunge. When this is done on a reliable lunge horse by an experienced trainer, the rider should be able to concentrate entirely on their position, relinquishing responsibility for guiding the horse. Riding without reins and stirrups for some of the time is great for these exercises. It can be very telling, when riding without stirrups and holding the hands in the position of holding the reins, how much the hands inadvertently move. In the beginning, it is best for the rider to either use the pommel of the saddle to hold onto, or a neck strap, for safety and to help pull themselves deeper into the saddle when practising without stirrups. This should not be practised for too long at once until the rider's balance and muscles are accustomed to it. When the stirrups are taken back, the reins can still be left alone, and the rider can then concentrate on keeping the hands steady.

Figure 3.5 Rider Just Off Lunge Practising Leg-Yield
Note the brilliant classical seat and light rein contact. Photo courtesy of Brian and Lesley Skipper.

A good seat can be attained without lunge lessons, but it is far more difficult, will take longer and is likely to be harder on the horse's mouth.

The three-point seat

The three-point seat is a widely accepted principle of the classical seat. This means that the seat should be distributed equally on either seat-bone with a small amount of weight in the crutch area. (See Sylvia Loch's book *The Classical Seat* [Ref: 3.1] as well as many of her other books.) This principle is sometimes misunderstood to mean that the rider is putting weight onto the pubic bone. This, of course, is not what is meant, and it would be impossible. It simply means putting a little weight onto the front area of the seat and is not the same as sitting 'on the fork'.

As established, the rider's seat actually includes the groin and inner thigh areas, not just the buttocks. It is important that we sit on the strongest part of the horse's back, around the fourteenth vertebrae, which is just behind the withers, as instructed by Xenophon. So, it is important that our weight is kept in the centre of the saddle, as near to the pommel as possible, and not allowed to slide to the back of the saddle (the weakest part of the horse's back), as seen in the 'chair seat'. Here is an extract from Sylvia's book *The Rider's Balance* published by Kenilworth Press (Ref: 3.2):

> How many riders realise that we cannot be stable in the saddle unless the entire underside of the seat is in contact with the saddle to a greater or lesser degree? Rocking onto the seat bones and losing contact in front will destabilise the whole structure above and below the waist. Perching on the fork and losing contact through the buttocks blocks the rider's back and will place the horse on the forehand.

It normally takes months to develop the ability to sit astride a horse with hips wide enough apart to facilitate a deep independent seat. There are exercises off the horse that can help. Raising a straightened leg from the hip in front of the body and to the side is one example as long as it is done gently to begin with. There are several ligaments in the human groin area which need to be stretched in order for the hips to be opened to the optimum degree. Stretching exercises must be done slowly and carefully, and the amount of extension must be gradually built up (just as we would with our horse) in order to avoid injury. There are various popular exercise techniques, such as yoga, Pilates, and the Alexander technique, all of which will help to achieve suppleness for riding.

The classical seat for jumping and cross country

The deep classical seat described previously is not appropriate on all occasions. On a young or unmuscled horse, the rider should not sit so deeply but take more weight onto the thighs, knees and stirrups until the horse's back is strong enough to take the full seat.

Also, the upper body position will need to be adjusted for other activities, such as galloping across country and jumping; however, the basic principles remain the same: a straight line from the rider's head, shoulder, hip and heel, keeping the rider over the horse's centre of balance, which has been taken forward, as has the rider's upper body.

Up the body – down the weight

Returning to the deep seat: -

This is one of the mottos of the Spanish Riding School. It means that the rider should, whilst flatwork schooling, sit proud and tall from the waist up

Figure 3.6 The Late Peter Robeson, OBE

Here is another photo of the late Peter Robeson OBE. (See previous photo in Chapter 1, Fig. 1.5). Note the rider's seat just above the saddle, ready for the rider to sit upright on landing and resume the classical seat, without any pounding into the saddle. The horse being given optimum chance to stretch, with the hands either side of the neck, rather than on the mane. – Image courtesy of Alamy.com.

and allow the weight to sink from the waist downwards. With the rider's head erect, chin slightly in towards the chest, there should be a straight line between the rider's head, shoulders, hips and heel, as mentioned earlier.

These instructions may be relatively easy to achieve at the halt; it is when the horse and rider are moving when things become more difficult. The rider needs to be able to have the right amount of 'give' in the lower back to absorb the movement, whilst still keeping the torso proud and upright.

The instruction often given today to 'go with the horse' is usually interpreted to mean move the buttocks back and forth in an exaggerated motion, which causes a grinding effect on the horse's back. It sometimes has an effect on the rider's shoulders as well as the arms and hands, causing a lot of unnecessary and damaging movement. Sadly, many trainers praise this type of movement

Figure 3.7 A Non-Classical, Bad Jumping Position

This rider is completely out of balance, not over the centre of gravity and 'before' the horse's movement. She has launched herself into the air, and it is not a harmonious sight. The reins are tight, and the horse will not have the freedom to stretch his neck over the jump. Photo by Lesley Skipper.

and sometimes even say 'brush the saddle with your seat-bones'. I'm afraid this will impede the horse's forward impulsion (which usually means the rider will drive hard with the legs), and in time, it could damage the horse's back. It is also bad for the human spine. Instead, the thing to do is to expand the chest and hold the upper body firm without stiffness with a feeling of a slightly advancing waist, which advances with each stride of the horse but only moves as much as the horse moves the rider.

To prove the safety of the classical seat

Ask a friend to stand in front of your horse when you're mounted and to hold each rein near the horse's mouth, being careful not to touch the horse's mouth – just leave the horse's end slack. You hold the reins as normal and sit with collapsed tummy muscles, slightly slouching. Ask your friend to suddenly pull the reins forward as the horse may do, say when stumbling (they should be careful not to pull so hard as to pull you off!). You will

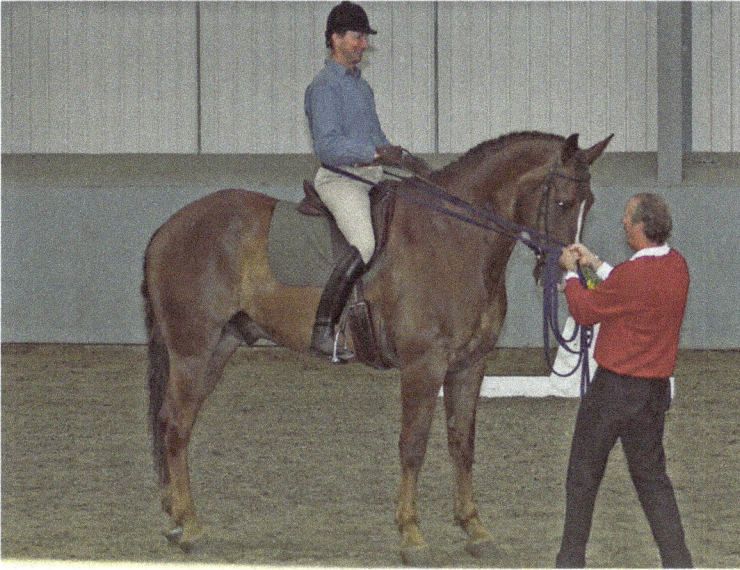

Figure 3.8 Confirming the Classical Seat

Here you can see the rider being gently pulled forward from the waist, and it is quite easy, when in the true classical position, to stay firm and upright. It's easy to imagine being violently pulled forward if in any other position. Photo courtesy of Paul Belasik.

doubtless be violently pulled forward over the horse's neck. Then try the same thing as you sit tall with expanded chest and strong abdominals. Your forward thrust will be greatly diminished. If you are sitting correctly, the difference will be startling. This is how the classical seat can help to keep the rider in the saddle in times of trouble, instead of falling off over the horse's neck or shoulder, which is a very common way to fall. Classical training will greatly enhance the balance of both horse and rider as the rider will be over the horse's centre of balance, making it easier for both parties. It will also greatly enhance the horse's responsiveness, and the horse/rider combination will be a lot safer. The horse is less likely to trip or fall if the rider is in balance.

References

Ref: 3.1 – 'The Classical Seat – The Key to Great Riding' (Paperback) – Loch, Sylvia – Horse & Rider Publication – 2011.

Ref: 3.2 – 'The Rider's Balance – Understanding the Weight Aids in Pictures' – Loch, Sylvia – Kenilworth Press – 2018.

Contact with the horse's mouth   4

The contact with the horse's mouth is one of the most difficult things to describe since it is slightly different with each horse and varies with each stage of training of that horse. The aim, of course, is to have 'reins of silk', but it may take many years before that can be obtained. In the meantime, a horse in training needs the help and support from the reins, but that is not the same as the rider pulling on the reins.

There appear to be some deplorable practices in the teaching of riding these days. Sometimes pupils are told they should have so many pounds of weight in the reins and that to be 'put on the bit', the horse should have his nose pulled in towards his chest. This is unbelievably harmful!

Generally speaking, a horse in the early stages of training needs a firmer contact from the rider's hands than one who is able to move with more self-carriage and utilise his back and hind legs better. We talk of the horse being 'on the forehand' when a large proportion of his weight is carried by his front legs with his hind end 'bringing up the rear'. This, of course is a natural way for an untrained horse to move, particularly when carrying the extra weight of the rider, but being 'natural' does not make it good in the long term. Horses who are never taught classical dressage movements often spend their lifetime dragging themselves and their riders along with their front legs because they never learn how to lift their backs and use their hind legs properly. This results in unnecessary pressure on the front end, making the horse more susceptible to tripping, slipping, and the early onset of arthritis, not to mention tendon and ligament strain of the forelegs and back strain.

Horses, left to their own devices and never ridden or worked, do spend most of their lives on the forehand, which does not do them any favours,

DOI: 10.1201/9781003503422-5

Figure 4.1 Rein Contact

Here we see Secret in the relatively early stages of training (although not novice) working nicely in a Pelham bit with double reins (which should always be used with this bit, as opposed to roundings, whenever possible). There is a definite contact with the horse's mouth, but the reins are held sympathetically and move forward and back to 'give' with each stride. The horse is not being held inwards. Photo by Lesley Skipper.

but this extra weight on the forehand whilst ridden is much worse given the extra weight of the rider.

Whilst horses not being ridden can and do take weight back onto the quarters, during certain movements (usually for very short durations), they need to have a lot of help to build the strength and flexibility to do so whilst carrying a rider.

I quote from Col. Alois Podhajsky's *Complete Training of Horse and Rider* (Ref: 4.1):

> Contact will depend on the conformation and temperament of the horse. Horses with weak hindquarters, which develop a greater pushing than carrying force, will in most cases have too strong a contact. . . . In most cases this will be due to a dullness or general stiffness of the horse, or a consequence of incorrect training.

We should be extra patient in the early days of training. The rider should support the horse with the hands when needed. By 'support', I don't mean pulling – just a gentle but firm guide to help him. When the horse is able to lighten the feel on the bit, the rider may lighten the feel by slightly opening

Figure 4.2 Needing Light Support

Here we see Secret in action needing light support. Photo by Lesley Skipper.

Figure 4.3 A Few Steps in Self-Carriage

Here we see Secret again at the same stage of training beginning to take a few steps in self-carriage without the need of support from the rider's hands. This may only happen momentarily to begin with. Photo by Lesley Skipper.

Figure 4.4 Secret When Just Backed

Secret's nose is well in front of the vertical. I make no attempt to pull her nose in. My leg is a bit too far back in this shot. Photo by John Wilson.

the fingers. At first these moments of lightness may only be brief. If the horse feels the rider's sympathetic giving with the rein, then he will want to experience it again. Eventually, the amount of time that he can feel lighter in the rider's hands will gradually be built up.

The amount of time taken for these early lessons is completely variable; each horse is different in temperament, conformation and so on. For instance, the Iberian breeds tend to find it very easy to take weight back onto the quarters and become light in hand, but we must be very aware in this case not to allow the horse to advance too quickly. It is often the case that this type of horse's training is hurried too much, and too much weight is taken back too early, damaging the joints, particularly the hocks.

With the heavier breeds, it is often a case of patience and more patience as their progress may seem slow; but make no mistake, patience will pay off in the end.

In these early lessons, the horse's nose is likely to be naturally well in front of the vertical due to his back being relatively weak and somewhat hollow. Our aim is to gently and gradually encourage flexion of the jaw and gullet, and the nose can then naturally assume a position nearer to the ideal, which is on or just in front of the vertical. It should never be forced there, and this will happen naturally only when the entire body of the horse is strengthened,

Figure 4.5 Secret Again Just Backed

Here is Secret again just backed, showing the gentle but firm support needed. Photo by John Wilson.

particularly the back, hind leg joints, hips, quarters and so on. The position of the head comes from correct training behind the saddle, hence the saying 'ride the horse from back to front', never the other way around.

As I keep saying, all horses are different. Some fairly thick-set horses are quite wide in the gullet and find it much more comfortable to keep their noses further in front of the vertical. This is fine as it is their conformation which is dictating this. It does not mean that they cannot be light in hand and strong and supple. It does not always follow that their backs are weak and hollow.

There are other horses who naturally bring their noses slightly behind the vertical or in towards the chest, and this too is perfectly acceptable as long as they are not encouraged to do this and they are not doing this to avoid the bit, that is, 'going behind the bit'. Carrying the nose just slightly behind the vertical does not necessarily mean that the horse is 'dropping the bit'.

Behind the bit

In the case of horses perpetually going behind the bit (and the contact with the mouth being lost), then the bridle and bit itself should be examined.

Is there something about the bit which is uncomfortable, or even painful, which the horse is trying to avoid? When the bridle and/or bit is confirmed to be comfortable (and the horse's teeth checked), then the rider should look at their own hands and contact with the bit. When the rider has a light contact, the horse should be encouraged forward with the legs and encouraged to lengthen the neck. As long as there is no discomfort in the mouth, then the horse should learn to accept the bit with pleasure.

Going behind the bit can be caused by asking for collection too soon, when the necessary strength in back and quarters has not been obtained, or by the rider's hands being too strong. All these things should be considered and appropriate time and patience taken.

A horse leaning on one rein

In the case of the horse leaning one rein, the rider can intermittently open and close the fingers on that rein, or momentarily give away the contact altogether on that rein.

The horse not wishing to flex or bend in that direction is often leaning on one side. This can be helped by the rider using a gentle tapping leg aid on the leaning side in conjunction with the intermittent rein aid.

None of this should be interpreted as 'sawing' at the horse's mouth. Some riders will pull with one rein and then the other to the extent of moving the bit from side to side. It is known as 'sawing' and is detrimental in every way.

Rein and body aids when turning

Because of the 'through' effect of the rein, that is, the action of the rein having a direct effect on the hind legs, it is better, in the majority of cases, for the hands to be used as a pair. For instance, when turning to the right, the rider should take both hands to the right. This should be accompanied by the rider's shoulders and head turning to the right with an expanded chest. The right leg should be in contact with the horse at the girth as a pillar for him to turn around. Slightly more weight should be put into the right stirrup (therefore right seat-bone). At the same time the left (outside) leg slides slightly back from the hip in order to guard against the quarters swinging out to the left.

In this way the horse should make a balanced turn, stepping through especially with the inside hind leg, and without falling onto the right (inside) shoulder. If only the right (inside rein) is used, then the horse is bound to turn his head and neck too much with too much weight falling onto the inside shoulder. The turn would then be unbalanced, uncomfortable and, instead of stepping through under the body, the hind legs will be left trailing. More about this in Chapter 8.

In some cases, at the very elementary stages, when the horse is just backed, it may be necessary to use more inside rein – even an 'open rein' to make it clear to the horse that he needs to turn his neck in one direction – but care should be taken not to overbend the neck and not to abandon the outside rein altogether. The rider should just keep it gently 'there' against the neck so the horse is not pulled onto the inside shoulder.

On the bit

This is a much overused and misunderstood phrase. As mentioned before, the horse should put himself on the bit when he is ready, that is, when he is strong enough to reach further forward under his body mass with his hind legs. When he 'steps through' in this way, he can then flex his jaw through

Figure 4.6 Sylvia Loch and Prazer
Sylvia Loch with her Lusitano stallion Prazer, on the bit. Photo courtesy of Sylvia Loch.

the gullet and put himself onto the bit. He then accepts the bit, and the rider's rein contact, with pleasure.

Salivation from the mouth

If the horse yields to the bit only with the jaw and not the gullet, this can create a false impression of being on the bit. It is correct flexion of the jaw and the gullet which produces the desirable moist mouth. Individual horses will produce varying amounts of moisture, and this sometimes amounts to a thick lather. The moisture is produced by a gland in the gullet which is stimulated by the flexion, not by chewing on the bit as is sometimes thought.

In a fully trained horse, a dry mouth is usually a bad sign. In such cases, the correctness of the horse's acceptance of the bit and ability to step or reach through from behind should be scrutinised. Obviously, the suitability and comfort of the bit should be looked at.

In the case of a newly backed horse just coming into work, we would not expect to see much, if any, salivation from the mouth as he will not, as yet, be able to flex his jaw and gullet as required. Time must be allowed for his development in all respects, especially with a green horse.

In the case of a horse with an extremely tight, possibly 'crank' noseband (often accompanied by the head being forced back behind the vertical by artificial means, or very strong rein action), it is possible for the horse to have a great deal of saliva flowing from the mouth. This is possibly because he just cannot swallow properly, which is a deplorable situation, and obviously not from pleasurable acceptance of the bit. This type of saliva flow is not at all the same as the salivation which is produced from flexion of the gullet and jaw.

A brilliant source of further enlightenment on this subject is Sylvia Loch's DVD 'On the Bit' (Ref: 4.2).

The connection between seat and hands

It is widely accepted that good, quiet hands can only come from a good seat; however, this connection is often not fully understood.

Some very advanced classical riders who have impeccably quiet, deep seats are able to keep their hands perfectly steady, whilst at the same time following the movements of the horse, when their hands are held fairly high. It is quite acceptable and desirable for the rider's hands to be held higher whilst carrying out the higher airs, that is, when the horse is in quite a degree of collection and naturally has a higher head carriage, but it takes a good deal of skill on the part of the rider to reach this stage and years of training to prepare the horse. Such airs would be passage, piaffe and others.

For all stages of training leading up to this pinnacle of the art, the hands should be held slightly apart (about the same as the width of the bit) at the base of the neck or just above the withers. The aim should be to create a straight line from the rider's elbow down towards the horse's mouth. This straight line will not be a straight horizontal line from the elbow to the hand as this would cause a break in the straight line at the rider's hands, where the reins will naturally be angled downwards towards the horse's mouth. This seems to be a common mistake as rider's feel that the line from the elbow to their hand should be horizontal. This break in the line to the horse's mouth assuredly causes an uneven contact from the hand to the mouth. This is made much worse if accompanied by an unstable seat. Every time the seat bounces around, so will the hands, which must be dreadful for the poor horse! Another thing which seems to follow when the hands are held too high is that of one hand inadvertently being held higher than the other, which causes the bit to slant in the horse's mouth. In this unstable position, every time a turning aid is required, the hands are likely to flail all over the place. It is so much better to hold them low, at the base of the neck, where they may still be unstable but not as badly intrusive to the horse as when they are too high.

Length of rein

Many riders, who may be aware of all that's been discussed so far, in an attempt to be kind to the horse, have their reins too long. Whilst this does not cause a constant pull on the horse's mouth, it is far more likely to result in frequent jabs to the mouth when contact is made.

Everyone has to learn and develop a good seat; it doesn't happen overnight, and in the process, the hands are inevitably going to be less stable. During this process, there is nothing wrong with supporting the hands by touching the horse's neck either side of the withers, or using a neck strap.

Upper body posture

I must repeat the importance of the entire body: one cannot talk about hand and rein contact without body posture – the two are intrinsically intertwined. An important thing to bear in mind at all times is to sit tall with shoulders back and down in a relaxed manner rather than forced and stiff.

It is essential to expand the chest and develop toned abdominal muscles. Toned muscles are strong without causing tension. Strong core muscles will keep the rider upright, in balance and safe and allow the hands to be quiet.

The rider's head

The head should be held erect, firm but not stiff, with the chin slightly drawn back. It is important that the rider look between the horse's ears; always look where you want your horse to look. Some nervous or novice riders have a tendency to look downwards. Since the head is a very heavy part of the human body, this seriously disrupts their balance and affects the distribution of their weight in the saddle. It also tends to make the rider's shoulders hunched.

Maestro Nuno Oliveira always had a tendency to look down at his horse. I think this was in deep concentration on his horse, but he did not tilt his head to one side. In any case, he was such a genius, wonderful horseman in other ways, so he is allowed this one fault!

Conclusion

If all of the principles described in this chapter, and in Chapter 3, have given the rider a good, quiet and independent seat, it should then be quite possible to acquire good, quiet hands. An independent seat means that the rider will not be at all reliant on the reins for stability and can think about giving and taking with every stride of the horse, closing the fingers momentarily when necessary and giving through the back and elbows as the horse moves forward.

As mentioned previously, giving through the back does not mean rocking back and forth, nor an exaggerated push with the seat, which would cause driving with the buttocks onto the horse's back. Just a gentle movement in the small of the back as the horse moves forward will create a give with the reins with each stride.

References

Ref: 4.1 – 'The Complete Training of Horse and Rider' – Podhajsky, Col. Alois – Translated by Eva Podhajsky & Col. V.D.S. Williams – Harrap – 1967.

Ref: 4.2 – 'On the Bit' – DVD – Loch, Sylvia – Available from Sylvia Loch, Long Meadow, Tilbury Juxta Clare, Sudbury, CO9 4JT.

The halt and half-halt   **5**

The halt

To ask the horse to come to a halt is one of the most basic and necessary of aids, and one of the most misused.

Many experienced riders do it very badly. Many riding schools and, I'm sad to say, advanced trainers teach it badly. Yet, it is so easy to do it well! It is one of the first things which separates the good, classical riders from the rest.

In the early stages of training, we are not expecting an abrupt square halt. We are merely asking that the horse comes to a halt in a balanced way, from walk, without falling onto the forehand. This may entail slowing the walk for two or three strides first, until the horse is a little stronger and can halt more immediately in walk.

Rider's aids for the halt

The first thing to do is to 'grow taller'; even though you should be sitting erect anyway, you should slightly brace your back (holding you're your back and tummy muscles in slight tension). Push the small of your back slightly forward, advancing your hips at the same time, pushing your tummy forward.

At the same time as you advance your hips, your upper inner thighs should close against the horse, thus having an arresting feel to the forward movement. Whist in motion, the inner thighs should lie as flat as possible against the saddle, without gripping, and allowing the movement to flow

DOI: 10.1201/9781003503422-6

Figure 5.1 Secret in Early Training
Here is Secret in very early training (still in a snaffle bridle). This is a good halt for a young horse. The feet are almost square, and she has not fallen too much onto the forehand. Note: her nose is still way in front of the vertical as would be expected at this stage of training. Photo by Lesley Skipper.

through. Now, when you want the horse to slow down or stop, is the time to tense these muscles whilst advancing your hips.

All that should be required from the reins is a gentle 'feel' to back up the request to cease the forward movement. This should be done fractionally after the other aids. When the horse is fully conversant with the body aids for halt, then it is very easy to halt without touching the reins.

The effects on the horse will be that the weight of the rider's seat will be eased from the back, more towards the front of the saddle. This will allow and encourage the horse to step through with the hind legs into the halt without dropping his back or falling onto the forehand. The closing of the thighs will indicate the cessation of forward movement. As soon as the halt is achieved, these aids should cease.

If you practise these steps, you will be amazed how easily your horse will come to a halt; even a newly backed horse will understand these aids because they are following the laws of nature.

Figure 5.2 Secret Relaxing at Halt

Here is Secret relaxing at the halt, but this is at a much later stage of training. Secret is more collected with a stronger back. Photo by Lesley Skipper.

The use of the voice is obviously very helpful in teaching the halt. This is quite reassuring to the horse. Just use the same vocal aid as you did in early leading and lunging.

The laws of nature

The reason that these aids are so easy for the horse to follow is because we are helping the horse to do what comes naturally. To come to a balanced halt, he needs to advance his back legs and hips. This is what we are helping him to do by advancing our hips, pushing our tummy forwards and lifting our weight slightly from the back of the saddle.

In all our riding, the horse and rider should mirror each other – shoulder to shoulder and hip to hip.

A very good way of understanding the aids for halt is to walk on foot with your hands on your hips. Walk normally in an upright position, and then come to a halt. If you come to a balanced halt, you will feel how your hips advance. You can try it without advancing your hips, and you will feel how your upper body will tip forward in a very unbalanced way. It is exactly the same for the horse. He will tip forward onto the forehand if he doesn't advance his hips.

It really is as simple as that. The horse does not need to learn by rote; it is a very natural thing.

The halts that go wrong

The halt will go wrong, or be extremely difficult and unbalanced, if the rider merely pulls on the reins, or if they lean back.

Many riders, even advanced dressage riders, seem to think that leaning back will help. It does exactly the opposite, and it is amazing that some advanced horses still manage reasonable halts even with this kind of hampering action of the rider. Leaning back will force undue weight onto the horse's back and make it extremely difficult for him to step through with his hind legs. Added to which, the act of slightly leaning back and pushing with the seat-bones (providing not done in excess) is a bone fide aid for forward movement much later in training. How confusing and uncomfortable it must be to have this conflicting aid, combined with a pull on the mouth!

To encourage the horse to stand square

When the horse is very young, unmuscled or untrained, we would not necessarily expect him to come to a square halt, that is, front and back legs parallel to each other. Some horses seem to do this naturally, whilst it is quite common for some to leave one hind leg trailing behind.

To help the horse in this regard, close your lower legs slightly back on the horse's sides. Just a little further back than the normal 'on the girth' position. Don't close your legs vigorously, and be careful not to nudge or otherwise give a forward aid at the girth. You should have a feeling of just gathering the horse's hind legs underneath him.

To begin with, you should be pleased with a reasonably (although not perfectly) square halt.

As the horse becomes established in coming to a balanced halt easily, then you can begin to request that his legs are square. It is normally one of the hind legs which is left behind. If his front feet are not square, then it is a good idea to ask him to walk on again and try another halt. Once the front feet are level, you can request that he 'steps up' with whichever hind leg is behind. You do this by gently taking your leg on that side back, and using it very discreetly, so he doesn't think he has to move forward.

It is sometimes helpful to have a friend on the ground to help by tapping or touching the leg which is behind.

It also makes sense, in the beginning, to always make your halts on the track in order to keep the horse straight. When asking the horse to 'step up' with a trailing hind leg, it is much better to have halted with this leg on the inside of the school so he is not tempted to move sideways; the wall of the school will be there to deter this.

When to ask for a halt

The halt is obviously a necessary request from the earliest of training. When it is first asked under saddle, as mentioned previously, we are not asking for perfection, merely for the horse to halt in as balanced a way as he is capable, and when necessary. Do not practise the halt very often when the horse is newly backed. Later in training, when he is stronger, then a more correct halt can be requested, perhaps twice during a training session, but never overdo it. Repeated halts are strenuous and can be used as a reprimand, which can result in halts being resented by the horse.

Later on in training, perhaps when lateral work is being taught, the halt can become part of the general exercises practised daily, but even then, halting should not be overdone. A correct halt is very beneficial in many ways, and it is essential later on when training the rein-back.

To rein-back correctly is a very strenuous and advanced exercise, and I would not recommend this until lateral movements are well established and the horse has a degree of collection. That's why I am covering the rein-back later in this book. You should definitely not try rein-back until a correct halt is easy to obtain.

A good halt can only be expected from the walk in the early days, but much later in training, when the horse is capable of collection and strong in the haunches, it can be practised from the trot and eventually even the canter – but never try this too soon. When first practising it, say in trot, a few strides of walk should be expected before the actual halt; then these strides can be gradually reduced until the horse can fairly easily halt from the trot (see Chapter 15 for a discussion on halt transitions).

Whilst strength is needed to produce a good halt, much strength can be built up in the quarters by practising it in the right way, at the right time. It is better to err on the side of caution if you're not sure if your horse is ready, and leave it for some time. Too many bad halts can be harmful and are definitely harmful if the rider is using the wrong aids.

Here is an excerpt from the great master Francois Robichon de la Guérinière's book *School of Horsemanship* (Ref: 5.1):

> The advantages to be drawn from a well-executed halt are to collect the horse, lend support to its mouth, head and haunches, and to make it light to the hand. But just as much as halts are good when done properly, they are harmful when performed at the wrong moment.

What Guérinière says here is obviously referring to the halt as it is used in the fairly advanced training of the horse, when it is used to rebalance and build up strength in the hindquarters, not merely to stop. Nevertheless, it is far better, for both horse and rider, to learn how to do it properly at an early stage of training, even if perfection is not expected.

The Half-Halt

The half-halt is often a cause of confusion to experienced riders as well as new ones. It is, in fact, exactly what it says, almost a halt but not quite. There can be varying degrees of half-halt; sometimes the merest hint of an interruption in forward movement is all that is required.

It can be used to arrest the forward speed of a horse who is perhaps rushing. The forward impulsion is slightly interrupted by the aids for halt and then allowed to flow again – hopefully in a more sedate and balanced way.

It can usefully be used to rebalance the horse, that is, to ask for a little more weight to be taken back onto the haunches, or when the horse has simply become unbalanced. It can be very useful to prepare the horse just before a new exercise, say a lateral movement. It warns him of something different to come, rebalances his weight slightly backwards, and shortens his stride.

It is also invaluable when show jumping or riding cross country to rebalance the horse in between jumps or before a bend.

These half-halts can vary from a light check on the outside rein – say, if the horse is leaning slightly on that shoulder – to the full gambit of half-halt aids. The halt aids are given momentarily and then released, followed by impulsion aids – a feeling of almost halting, but then you don't.

The half-halt can be useful sometimes instead of an actual halt.

As mentioned previously, too many halts, especially abrupt halts, can be perceived by the horse as a punishment. It is the same with the half-halt. I feel that many trainers and riders overuse the half-halt – it should be used with discretion. A very young or untrained horse may be confused and upset by it.

Depending on how they are used, as well as how sympathetically they are ridden, the halt and half-halt can be either good exercises or a demoralising subjugation for the horse.

The aids for the half-halt

The aids for the half-halt are exactly the same as for the halt. The main difficulty, especially for the novice rider, is to learn to release these aids quickly enough, and then to give a forward aid. If these two aids are not separated, then they will conflict with each other, and the horse will be upset. When the rider is first learning the half-halt, it is preferable for the horse to very nearly halt before the forward aid is then given, and obviously only in walk. This will be much less upsetting to the horse than receiving the aids simultaneously, providing, of course, it is not practised repeatedly.

The horse himself, of course, has to learn to understand what is being asked. At first it must be quite confusing, but given time, patience and empathy, the movement can become smooth and helpful, and he will be able to rebalance a little weight backwards, which will help him. If the horse seems too confused or even annoyed, then it is best to leave the half-halt until later in training.

My advice generally is never to overuse the half-halt at any stage of training.

Reference

Ref: 5.1 – 'School of Horsemanship' – de la Guérinière, Francois Robichon – Translated by Tracy Boucher – J.A. Allen – 2003.

The walk and trot 6

Including rising and sitting trot, walk on a long rein, and the nodding head syndrome

The walk

Sequence of footfalls at the walk

The walk is a four-time beat and very different from the trot or canter. Each foot moves independently, and there are always at least two feet on the ground at any time. It can be quite a 'rolling' gait.

There are three basic walks recognised in dressage today: collected, medium and extended. Medium walk is the horse's natural walk. This is the walk which he should perform at the earliest stages of training, without needing help from the rider. Providing he is striding out in a rhythmic, unhurried, yet purposeful way, then my advice is leave well alone. It is very easy to ruin the rhythm of a good natural walk by trying to extend or collect too soon. Collected and extended walks are something which can be practised later in training. The main things to strive for now (in the early stages of training), and in fact throughout the training, are relaxation, rhythm, impulsion and straightness. The rhythm of the walk is easily disturbed, more so than any other gait, so it must be preserved.

Extended strides in any gait should not be attempted until collection is attained.

A common mistake, even in the early stages of training, is to hurry the horse on in walk or trot. It is particularly damaging in walk. Many trainers and dressage judges have the misunderstanding that the walk should be

DOI: 10.1201/9781003503422-7

fairly fast and the horse should reach through with their hind legs, which is known as tracking-up (hind feet reaching the footfalls of the front feet). This is not so, especially in the early stages of training. A big horse may have what some onlookers may think is a lazy stride, but as long as there is true impulsion, that is, flexion of the joints, then speed is detrimental. Tracking-up will come with strength due to good training. It is also very dependent upon the conformation of the horse; although desirable, it is not essential. Tracking-up will be covered more fully in Chapter 14.

The forward aid

The forward driving aid from the rider should be a gentle nudge from the rider's inner calf muscles in the 'on the girth' position (Figure 3.3 shows 'on the girth' position). If this appears unsuccessful, then sometimes a gentle vibratory aid from the inner side of the boot may excite the horse into action. As soon as the horse has responded, the aid should be ceased. It is in the cessation of an aid that the horse learns that he is doing what is required. There must be nothing more disheartening for the horse than a rider who constantly nudges or kicks with the heels. It usually leads to the horse completely ignoring the aid or, worse still, becoming 'dead to the leg'. Whether the nerve endings on the horse's sides have become physic- ally damaged and deadened by this constant attack, or whether the horse mentally blocks it out, is not known. In any event, it is a horrible scenario.

Another result of continuous driving aids is that it has a detrimental effect on the rider's position, usually causing the seat to be completely destabilised with a knock-on effect to the rest of the torso.

There is a series of what are known as intercostal nerves, which pass between the muscles lying between the ribs. They lie very close to the sur- face, and, conveniently for us, every time the rider's legs touch the horse's sides, these intercostal nerves affect the horse's back muscles (see Figure 6.1). Exciting these nerves by gently tapping the horse's sides is how we ask the horse for forward movement. See Chapter 13 for precise positioning of the leg for the impulsion aid.

Many trainers instruct their pupils to squeeze with both legs as an aid for forward impulsion. There are two very good reasons why squeezing is not good. I quote from *Exercise School for Horses* by Lesley Skipper (Ref: 6.1):

> Riders are often told to squeeze the horse's sides with their legs. This presumably came about as an antidote to the idea of kicking in order to get the horse to move. While kicking is certainly unpleasant for the

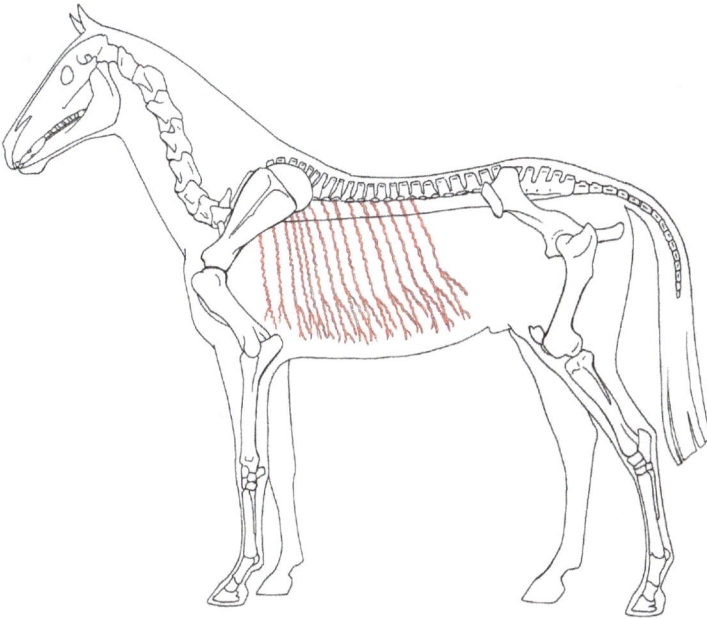

Figure 6.1 Intercostal Nerves

This shows the intercostal nerves lying just below the surface of the horse's sides. They affect the horse's back muscles. See Chapter 13 for precise placing of the leg aids for different movements. Figure courtesy of Lesley Skipper.

horse, squeezing can be equally so, as well as being ineffective. The horse's lungs lie almost directly below the area where the rider's legs act, so any constriction in this area is bound to affect his breathing. There is another, very good reason why squeezing is counter-productive. I imagine most of us have, at some time or another, sat for some time in a position which results in numbness in one or both legs. This numbness comes about because of continuous pressure on the leg nerves.

I would imagine that this contributes towards the 'dead to the leg' scenario.

The pushing aid of the seat should not be used in the early stages of training.

The action of the horse's head in the walk is far more pronounced than in the trot. In the walk, the head moves back and forth and, to some extent, side to side. It varies with the conformation of the horse. This action should be allowed for and followed by the rider's hands. A gentle but constant contact can be kept by the rider's give and take through the elbows and lower back. In some cases, it may be necessary for a quick 'give' with alternate reins to allow for the movement of the head from side to side. This can be done by just slightly opening the fingers momentarily on that rein.

The whip

Any driving aid should not need to be forceful or harsh. If gentle aids do not appear to have any effect, then a tap with the whip near the leg is far preferable than continued or hard driving leg aids or kicking.

The whip should always be seen as a friendly aid – an extension of the rider's body. He should have become accustomed to the friendly whip aid long before backing – in hand and on the lunge.

If your horse is frightened of the whip, then the likelihood is he has been abused by it in the past. It will take quite some time to retrain him into understanding that he is not going to be 'hit' by the whip. It can be done with time and patience – in hand to begin with, using treats to reward him when he allows the whip to touch him (not as bribes beforehand). Ultimately, you should be able to stroke all over his body with the whip without any apprehension on the part of the horse. After this, then the whip can be used as it should be, that is, as an aid to help the horse understand what is required.

Walk on a long rein

Allowing the horse to stretch out in the walk on a long rein is most desirable before, frequently during and after any schooling sessions. Muscles which are going to work, and therefore contract, first need to stretch. It is not always possible if the horse is excited or tense, but it is definitely something we should aim for.

In cold weather, it is probably advisable to use an exercise sheet as a cold wind will not facilitate a feeling of relaxation in the horse.

The idea is that the horse will stretch his head and neck forward and down. It does not mean giving away the rein contact completely. You should gradually feed out the reins through softly 'feeling' fingers. At the same time, although this is a time of relaxation, the horse should not be slouching along. He should not be rushed, but he should be encouraged by gentle leg aids to step through from behind so he is not just allowing his weight to fall onto the forehand. He should stay on a gentle hand contact.

The horse will dictate the amount he wishes (or is comfortable) to stretch. The rider suggests the stretching by lowering the hands either side

Figure 6.2   Stretch on Long Rein
Here we see my horse Lucy relaxed but walking actively, stretching her neck and back muscles, during a break from work. Photo by Horsepix.

of the withers. Young, tense or stiff horses will not find this stretching easy, nor comfortable to begin with, but as training progresses, they should find it easier and welcoming.

The horse should never be pulled downwards, nor inwards.

Taking time to allow this stretching, even if it is minimal to start with, will pay dividends in the end. Giving the horse plenty of relaxation time in between work will help him to enjoy his work, and he will be more able to perform well. It promotes blood flow through the muscles and removes toxins.

During these relaxation periods, the rider should not neglect their own position; stay upright and keep the tummy forward without slouching at the waist.

Free walk on a long rein should not be confused with deep work, which is quite different. I do not propose to describe that here, as it is not always necessary, and to practise it correctly takes a lot of skill. If done incorrectly, it can be damaging, so I think it is best left to the classical masters.

Deep work should also not be confused with rollkur, or hyperflexion of the head and neck, which is always extremely detrimental.

Walk work prior to trotting

Walk work is generally very undervalued. There are so many exercises which can be carried out in walk, including circles, turns, serpentines and demi-pirouettes, not to mention the lateral work, such as leg-yield, and later on in the training, shoulder-in, half-pass and so on. There are also transitions to and from the halt, so long as this is not done to excess as the halt can be construed as a punishment by the horse if practised in excess. There is no need for walk work to be boring. All these exercises, once the horse is warmed up, can be interspersed so the horse never knows what will be asked of him next. It is interesting for both horse and rider when the rider concentrates on their position, weight aids and so on and endeavours to carry out each movement with precision. There is nothing at all wrong with spending the whole schooling session time in walk when first building up the strength in the horse's back. The back can, and does, build up very well in walk, if necessary, without trotting.

Of course, sometimes the horse may be exuberant, in which case a spell of trot work may be necessary just to satisfy his needs.

The trot

Sequence of footfalls in the trot

The trot consists of a two-time beat with the legs moving in diagonal pairs. There are always two feet (a diagonal pair) on the ground at any one time. The sequence is as follows: right hind and left fore together, and then left hind and right fore together, commencing with either diagonal.

The great master Col. Alois Podhajsky, in his book *Complete Training of Horse and Rider*, noted the following (Ref: 6.2):

> Throughout the whole training of the horse, including the first phase, the trot plays the most important role in the work. It is better qualified than any other pace to make the young horse supple and flexible, to teach obedience, and to make the paces more rhythmic and regular.

Rising trot

The rising trot is the mainstay of the trot work in the early stages of training, as well as during the warm-up period for the whole of the horse's life. It is also good to intersperse some rising trot in between the sitting trot work to relieve the horse's back briefly.

In Sylvia Loch's book *Dressage in Lightness*, she notes the following (Ref: 6.3): "Rising trot encourages the build-up of rhythm in the trot by freeing the horse's back, particularly during the moment of suspension".

I'd just like to mention here that, personally, I found the rising trot impossible to do for a year or two before, and following, knee replacement surgery. Some months after the surgery, I was able to resume rising again, but for quite some time, my horse and I had to be content with sitting trot only. To compensate for this inability, I did far more warm-up and strengthening work in walk and kept the trot work for shorter durations than I would otherwise have done. I found this to be perfectly acceptable for my horse, but this is bearing in mind that she already had well built-up back muscles, and I am able to sit to the trot quite well without undue bouncing, causing little problem to her back.

Back to the rising trot

This is usually the first trot which both horse and rider are used to employing. Unfortunately, many riders are not taught particularly well. At

Figure 6.3 Sitting Trot
This shows Secret and I in the sitting phase of the rising trot. Photo by Lesley Skipper.

Figure 6.4 Rising Trot

Here we are as I am just about to rise. Photo by Lesley Skipper.

Figure 6.5 Rising Phase of Rising Trot

Here I am in the rising phase of the rising trot. Note that my seat is not far out of the saddle (only as much as the horse pushes me), and my hips are slightly inclined forwards. Photo by Lesley Skipper.

the beginning of the rider's career, the instructor will usually call 'up-down, up-down'. This may be helpful for the rider to understand the rhythm of the trot, but it usually means that riders tend to launch themselves far higher out of the saddle than is necessary with the inevitable bang onto the saddle as the seat returns. Far too much effort tends to be put into leaving the saddle. It usually results in an ungainly, unbalanced picture of horse and rider struggling to keep 'with each other'. It is extremely harmful to both horse and rider and is not necessary.

I would much prefer the rider to have the instruction (and feeling) of 'forward-back', rather than 'up-down'. How much the seat should leave the saddle is, of course, entirely dependent upon the trot stride and conformation of the horse. Some horses have big, bouncy strides, so the rider's seat will be pushed up higher by the action of the horse's back, but there is no need to exaggerate this. The rider should only leave the saddle as much as he is pushed up by the horse's movement.

Bring your upper body and hips forward slightly, keeping your upper body tall and abdominal muscles toned as you feel the thrust of the horse's diagonal legs move (you will feel this through the back). Come lightly back into the saddle on the next beat of the diagonal. It is a case of getting into the rhythm with the horse, and only practice will make perfect. In general, it is better to think of a forward and sit movement instead of up and down.

This is how Susan McBane describes it in her excellent book *100 Ways to Improve Your Riding* (Ref: 6.4):

> I find that the most effective way is for the back to remain flat as the rider brings the upper body forward from the hip joints, carrying the shoulders above the knees. In this position, the rise is much lessened and can be done subtly by just tilting the bottom of the pelvis forwards on one trot diagonal and letting it come back again (sitting lightly) on the next.

Some horses' conformation dictates that their trot is very smooth, in which case the thrust of the diagonal legs leaving the ground will be far less. In some cases, the height of the rider's seat leaving the saddle is barely discernible to the onlooker, and this is all to the good.

Rhythm

Rhythm is all important in riding, and each horse will have a slightly different rhythm, but it should be an even rhythm if the horse is sound.

Any unevenness, of course, would mean that the horse has a problem and is probably lame. The rider should be aware of this, and any unevenness should be investigated, especially if accompanied by nodding of the horse's head. It is usually in the trot where lameness is first detected.

Use of the ball of the foot

The rider should use slight pressure from the ball of the foot on the stirrup to instigate the rise. This will avoid gripping with the legs, which would give conflicting signals to the horse and destabilise the rest of the rider's position.

The legs should be almost motionless against the horse's sides, neither gripping nor banging. Because of the motion of the horse, there will nearly always be a modicum of movement, but this should be minimal.

Rising on the correct diagonal

Riders will be rising when one pair of legs is in the air and moving forward, and sitting when the opposite pair is on the ground. Most riders, and horses, have a preferred diagonal, in other words, without thinking about it, the rider will rise on a certain diagonal naturally, practically every time. This is because of human and equine natural 'one-sidedness', which we strive to minimise in our training.

When out hacking on a straight line, it matters little which diagonal the rider is rising on, save for the fact that it is actually better to change it occasionally to prevent the perpetual loading of one particular hind leg and neglecting the other, thereby exacerbating the one-sidedness.

However, when riding turns, circles or in a school, where there are of course constant turns, it is far better to be sitting when the outside shoulder is coming back. This means that the inside hind leg is the one receiving most of the weight. This concurs with the laws of nature and balance. To be in good balance, both horse and rider should have slightly more weight to the inside of any bend or circle.

The outside shoulder is, of course, always the one on the outside of the bend.

I think most people find it easiest to check which diagonal they are on by glancing down at the horse's shoulder. You should be sitting when the outside shoulder is coming back.

Obviously, you should be rising when the inside shoulder comes back – same thing, just a different way of checking.

When checking the diagonal, try to glance down with your eyes only, as tilting the head will unbalance your whole body since the head is a proportionately heavy part of the body.

Changing diagonals

When riding in the arena, we need to change diagonals frequently, each time we change the rein. To do this, we must either sit for two beats (which I find easiest) or stay out of the saddle for two beats. Whichever way you choose to do it, at first you may end up sitting or out of the saddle for three beats instead of two, thus returning to the same diagonal. So, check which shoulder is coming back and if it's wrong, just try again. With practice, it will become easier.

Sitting trot

Sitting trot should not be commenced until the horse is sufficiently strong in the back to take the full seat of a rider. How long this will take varies immensely. Obviously, for a young horse with a conformationally weak back, it will take a long time, possibly years. The age, fitness, conformation and size of the horse, along with size and weight of the rider, will all have a bearing on this.

The rider's ability to sit well with a secure, classical seat in the centre of the saddle, as near to the pommel as possible, with an upright torso and taking responsibility for their own weight will have a huge bearing on how much weight the horse will feel on his back.

Just imagine giving someone a 'piggy back' on your back. If the person you are carrying is moving and unstable, it is so much more difficult than if they sit still and upright.

If you are not sure whether you and your horse are ready for sitting trot, then it would be wise to consult an experienced classical trainer.

Whilst the trot itself is the mainstay of training, sitting trot is the mainstay of more advanced training. Most of the lateral exercises are carried out in sitting trot (it is possible to rise to the trot in shoulder-in), and things such as piaffe and passage cannot be done whilst rising.

The amount of movement in the small of the back

As mentioned before, the rider needs to be able to allow the small of the back to move gently back and forth as the horse rises and lands in the diagonal movement. In the sitting trot, this is most crucial. Care must be taken not to force this movement and not to push back and forth. Just move as the horse moves you. This is much easier on a horse with a slow, smooth trot. A jog trot is helpful for the rider at first to obtain the feel and relax enough with the seat and legs, keeping the upper body erect without tension. Of course, jog trotting is something which most trainers would discourage, but in the interests of training the rider, it is of immense help.

Lessons on the lunge without reins and stirrups are the best way to learn to sit the trot.

The nodding head syndrome

The nodding of the rider's head is quite a common sight in the dressage arena. It is not only ugly but injurious.

In this case, the rider has usually allowed their chest to become concave, more or less collapsed at the waist, with the chin pushed forwards. In this position, the rider's torso is not supporting the head and neck, and much damage can be done to their spinal column. This is why it is so important (and I keep reiterating the fact) that the rider should keep an upright torso, supported by toned abdominal and back muscles (without tension), an expanded chest, shoulders relaxed back and down, and chin slightly brought in towards the chest.

Toned but relaxed buttock muscles are essential in the sitting trot; tension in these muscles will cause bouncing and instability.

Once you have mastered a good sitting trot, you will find it helps in every other gait, including improving your rising trot.

Interspersing rising and sitting trot within a training session will be good for horse and rider. The change from sitting to rising and back again should be smooth with no change of rhythm.

References

Ref: 6.1 – 'Exercise School for Horse and Rider' – Skipper, Lesley – New Holland Publishers (UK) Ltd. – 2008.

Ref: 6.2 – 'The Complete Training of Horse and Rider' – Podhajsky, Col. Alois – Translated by Eva Podhajsky & Col. V.D.S. Williams – Harrap – 1967.

Ref: 6.3 – 'Dressage in Lightness – Speaking the Horse's Language' – Loch, Sylvia – J.A. Allen – 2000.

Ref: 6.4 – '100 Ways to Improve Your Riding – Common Faults and How to Cure Them' – McBane, Susan – David & Charles – 2004.

The canter

7

The sequence of footfalls of the canter

The canter is a three-time beat and very different from the walk and trot. The sequence of footfalls (when cantering on the left rein), are as follows: the right hind strikes off independently, then the left hind and right fore move together, followed by the left foreleg moving independently (the leading leg).

There are four different canters recognised in the dressage arena today: collected canter, working canter (normal or natural strides and the one you will mostly be using), medium canter and extended canter. These are further explained in Chapter 15.

There is a time in the stride where all the weight is taken by one hind leg, and there is a moment of suspension when there is no contact with the ground. It is the only dressage pace which has a definite right- or left-leading side. There is a degree of bend (although not too much), or at least flexion, in the direction of the leading leg. It is a definite skipping motion.

Cantering in an enclosed space such as a riding arena requires a degree of strength, balance and engagement of the hindquarters. Young or untrained horses often do not yet possess these attributes. It is much easier to canter first on a straight line whilst out hacking or in a field, which is what horses mostly do when free.

Even if you can see your horse cantering and cavorting, making turns and circles fairly easily in the field, it is a totally different situation when under saddle, when they have the weight of the rider to balance as well as

DOI: 10.1201/9781003503422-8

their own. The relatively unstable weight of the rider can often throw the horse completely off balance.

Natural gaits

Some horses do not have a natural preference for the canter. For instance, Arabians find the canter infinitely more natural and easier than the Iberian breed. Many pony breeds, such as Dales ponies, are bred with a preference to the trot, likewise the Normandy Cobs. Dales ponies were first bred to carry farmers up and down the Dales hills, so naturally, not much cantering was required. That's not to say that Dales Ponies cannot canter; once trained, they can canter very nicely, but it may take a little longer to acquire the skill in this gait. New Forest Ponies were bred for fast cantering and galloping through the forest, so their natural abilities are different. There are obviously differences within breeds; some horses just find canter under saddle more challenging. Often, it is the horses with high action in trot who find canter more challenging.

It is little wonder, then, that the canter is something many riders find difficult.

Figure 7.1 Free Canter

This is a young horse enjoying himself in canter naturally when free, but it is totally different and more difficult when the horse has to balance himself and his rider, especially in an enclosed space. Photo by Lesley Skipper.

Patience is an essential virtue

In my experience, many of these difficulties are made worse by lack of patience. It takes time to build up the strength, balance and confidence for the horse to canter comfortably in the school. In many instances, as soon as the horse is going nicely forward in walk and trot, they are asked to canter. When this does not happen successfully, the rider immediately considers this a problem. Very probably, all they need to do is wait until the horse is stronger and better balanced in the trot, on the circles and turns, and in the beginnings of other movements, such as leg-yield. These will improve balance and flexibility, at which point the horse is more likely to be able to canter easily in the school.

It is never a good idea to push the horse into canter from an exceptionally fast trot and then rush around the school in an unbalanced canter, merely in order to say that the horse can canter. This can do a lot of harm to joints and tendons, not to mention harm to the horse's confidence, and it is dangerous. At the beginning, the young or untrained horse may need to go into canter from a faster trot than normal. Whilst this is permissible at first, if it helps him, it should not be encouraged, and he should definitely not be forced into it. It is also sometimes best to allow the young or untrained horse to canter slightly faster than you would prefer at the beginning so long as it is not for too many strides, and certainly not for a whole circuit of the school. If the young horse is cantering fast out of fear or agitation, then he should be brought back to trot, and canter should be abandoned until he is better prepared. Cantering slowly is more strenuous, so we must endeavour to make things as easy and safe as possible.

Looking to the outside

I have sometimes seen instructors teaching riders to ask the horse to flex to the outside of the arena when cantering, supposedly to increase their flexibility. This is highly dangerous and completely against the principle of the inside bend, which is fundamental in all classical dressage training. They may also ask the rider to look to the outside, too, which again is totally wrong. The rider's shoulders and hips should always mirror that of the horse, and in the case of the canter, or any bend and circle work, the rider's inside shoulder should be very slightly back, depending upon the degree of the bend. The inside hip is forward and outside hip back; just as the horse's hips are. The rider should look where he wants the horse to look, that is, towards the bend of the circle.

Figure 7.2 Natural Collected Canter

This horse is cantering in a collected manner in a free and natural way. It is the Arabian stallion Nivalis, owned by Brian Skipper. Photo by Lesley Skipper.

Figure 7.3 Collected Canter Under Saddle

This is a good, collected canter with an excellent classical rider. Cantering slowly in a collected way like this is far more strenuous than fast cantering and requires excellent balance. Photo is of Katharine Duckitt with her Lusitano stallion Quem Foi. Photo by Lesley Skipper.

In Paul Belasik's wonderful book *Dressage for the 21st Century*, he notes the following (Ref: 7.1): "The principle of inside bend remains unshakeable because of its simple but important physics: it remains one of the most important cornerstones of classical dressage". However, having said all of this, sometimes it is permissible to 'allow' a very young horse to momentarily look to the outside as he strikes off. This may help his balance at this very early stage as he is unable to balance correctly. Sometimes untrained horses will do this as they strike off when at liberty. It is not something which should be encouraged, nor perpetuated, as it pushes far too much weight onto the forehand. Once horses are well trained and balanced, they will naturally look to the inside of the canter strike off even at liberty.

Counter-bend has been experimented with countless times throughout history and has always been without success.

Some 'natural' trainers these days seem to think, because horses in the wild (untrained and unbalanced) will sometimes move in a counter-bend, that this is desirable.

I must point out here that counter-bend is not at all the same as counter-canter or cantering on the wrong leg.

Following are some of the many reasons why the great riding masters throughout the centuries have emphasised the need for an inside bend:

1. When a horse is being ridden, he has a weight above his back which must be balanced, along with his own weight, and this changes the centre of balance, making it a much more crucial issue. This is not the same as the pregnant mare who carries her extra weight underneath her belly.
2. The horse running free in the wild is well enough balanced for his life-style. He can gallop away from predators and travel long distances to find food, water and shelter, but he is not required to trot or canter ten metre circles. In classical dressage, we do not seek to change the natural beauty of the horse, but we do seek to enhance it, and we can do this by systematic training, helping the horse to become more balanced.
3. Well trained, and therefore well balanced, horses cease their inclination to counter-bend even when free. For instance, whilst being loose schooled with no rider aboard and whilst wearing no tack, the well-trained horse will always bend in the direction of the arc he is travelling. He has learnt that this is a better, safer and altogether more balanced way for him to travel, and once he is strong enough, it is more comfortable.
4. If the horse moves with a counter-bend on a circle, the centre of gravity will move towards the inside foreleg – just the opposite of what is required and what is physically best for him in the long run. When moving with a correct inside bend on a circle, the centre of gravity is inclined towards the inside hind leg, requiring this leg to carry more weight and to be

brought further under the body – the whole purpose of work on the circle. The hind legs, when gradually strengthened through the correct exercises, are much more able to carry extra weight and less likely to suffer structural damage. Young and unmuscled horses may prefer to counter-bend because it is easier for them, but counter-bend is certainly not good for the horse. It encourages more weight onto the forehand and is usually the cause of much lameness and early onset of arthritic conditions. This principle applies in all gaits.

We must remember that natural is not always best. Wild or feral horses are very lucky if they reach their early teens, but more usually die around 10. We all aim for so much better than this for our horses in captivity. When trained correctly, they have much more comfortable, healthy and happy lives.

Having said all of this, it is best not to ask for too much bend in the strike off; just ask for flexion to the inside.

Nothing should ever be forced in training

Some horses actually need a degree of collection before they can canter under saddle confidently. Since collection requires a good deal of strength and flexibility of joints and tendons, this can take a considerable time to achieve, so in these cases, one must be very patient. None of this should be rushed if we want to give our horse the best chance of a long and healthy life. The horse will tell us when he is ready; we may ask for canter, but forcing it is neither kind nor advisable.

Bigger horses in general find cantering in an arena more difficult than the smaller breeds. It is far more daunting for them since the size of their stride will, of course, dictate that they reach the corner of the arena much sooner. It also follows that they find balance in the school much more difficult. They need to be afforded however much time they need – months or even years. It won't matter if the trot work proceeds way beyond the canter work. The training programme should not be set in stone and should be tailored to suit each particular horse.

On the lunge

Cantering on the lunge is a good introduction to cantering in the school, but of course, it does not take into account the weight of the rider, which,

Figure 7.4 Cantering on the Lunge

Here is my mare Secret in the initial stage of training. She is enjoying herself whilst cantering on the lunge but moving too fast and in an unbalanced way (she was certainly not asked to move that way). This would not be good for any length of time, but in short bursts, when she was excited, it did teach her how to balance on the circle. Eventually, when calm, the horse can canter for a few strides in a balanced way on the lunge without undue stress. Photo by Lesley Skipper.

as mentioned before, can make a huge difference. I do not think it is a good idea to introduce canter under saddle on the lunge as the continuous circle is too demanding and strenuous for the horse at this early stage whilst carrying a rider.

Any work on the lunge, with or without a rider, should be on as large a circle as possible and never for long periods of time. Lunge work is very strenuous.

Hacking

Cantering in a straight line whilst out hacking is a good way of introducing some horses to the canter under saddle, providing it can be done on good ground (not too hard, lumpy or deep and muddy). It is best to have the company of experienced horses so as to keep the pace steady, as we don't want this to deteriorate into a panicky gallop. The canter should be kept to very short spurts to begin with.

Baby steps to start with

Going back to the school: when you think your horse is ready for canter, just two or three strides is sufficient to begin with. The number of strides can be gradually increased so long as the horse is comfortable with it. This will build up strength and confidence. The quality of any canter is always improved by the strike off, never by continuous cantering.

Cantering on a given leg

Most horses, and people for that matter, have a preferred side to strike off for the canter. When cantering in an enclosed arena, the horse needs to be 'on the right leg', that is, the first leg to strike off is the outside hind, followed by the inside hind and outside foreleg together. The last leg to leave the ground is the inside fore, which is termed 'the leading leg'. When watched from the ground, this inside fore can be seen to move in advance of the outside fore. The horse needs to be on this inside lead in order to safely negotiate the turns, with the inside hind and outside fore grounding at the same time, giving stability on the bend in this three-beat stride.

Whilst in the saddle, the best way to check that your horse is on the correct lead is to glance down at the shoulder; the inside shoulder should be seen coming farther forward in advance of the outside one.

Cantering on the wrong leg

Cantering on the wrong leg is not to be confused with counter-canter, but it is common with untrained horses and can be dangerous when negotiating corners, so it must be addressed without stressing the horse. He is not just being awkward or difficult; he is just unbalanced and untrained. It is our job to put this right in as tactful a way as possible. It is always possible that he is just not ready for canter in the arena just yet.

Whilst out hacking, it matters little which leg the horse is cantering on (if he is travelling on a relatively straight line), and, just as with the preference for the rider to rise on a particular diagonal in trot, the horse will have a preferred leg to canter on. This, again, is because of his natural one-sidedness. It is nothing at all to worry about, but it is something to work on in our training to make the horse (and ourselves) more ambidextrous. In dressage terms, we are making him straight, that is, able to bend equally and evenly on both sides.

If the horse finds it difficult or almost impossible to strike off on one particular lead, then more time must be spent in building flexibility, balance and strength in the trot. The canter can then be returned to at a later date when the horse is better prepared.

However, the difficulty of striking off on a particular lead is most likely to be a fault of rider position or aids, and this needs to be addressed before further attempts are made. Frequently failed attempts at canter strike off can be very disheartening for both horse and rider and can create a phobia or fear, so it is best not to keep trying. Repeated attempts using the same technique are likely to render the same results. Taking a break from this will not impede the walk and trot work, and you can both come back to the canter with a fresh outlook.

It is always a good idea to have the horse checked out by a good, qualified specialist, such as an equine osteopath, chiropractor, or vet, who should be able to rule out any physical difficulties the horse may be having.

Rider's aids

The aids for canter are as follows (in this case, for strike off on the right lead; this would be reversed for the left lead): the rider's left (outside) leg is taken slightly back from the hip, not just from the knee;

then, the rider's right hip (inside) and seat-bone is advanced, which almost inevitably happens when the outside leg is taken back; and finally, the rider gives a nudge with the inner calf of the inside leg at the same time as keeping contact with the outside leg taken back behind the girth. This should help the horse to strike off with the outside hind. Care should be taken not to use too much pressure with the outside leg as this could cause the quarters to swing inwards, which would unbalance the horse badly.

The advancement of the inside hip is of paramount importance. The outside leg being taken back will automatically slightly lighten the outside seat-bone and deepen the inside seat-bone. This is important to enable the horse to push off with the outside hind and step under his body with this leg. He obviously needs to do this at every canter stride.

The rider's hands should gently support the horse and 'go with' any lengthening of the neck; the rider must not pull back in any way as this would hinder the strike off. Be careful not to abandon the horse's head as this can be quite frightening to a young horse. The outside rein should be held in gentle contact; too much give with this rein will unbalance the horse, especially on the turns.

Needless to say, the rider should be in a good classical position, taking responsibility for his own weight. It is sometimes helpful to ease the weight slightly off the horse's back in the very early stages, as in a forward seat (more weight onto knees, thighs and stirrups), but making sure that your chest is expanded and you are not collapsing at the waist, which would throw weight onto the horse's forehand. This forward seat is not always helpful to all horses. It may actually be off-putting to some, in which case, just make sure you keep your seat as still and light as possible, without losing the advancement of the inside hip.

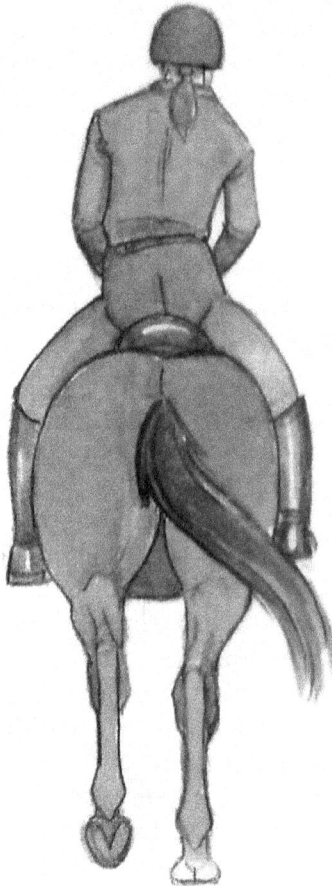

Figure 7.5 Collapsed Hip

This drawing is reproduced by kind permission of Sylvia Loch and Kenilworth Press from the book *The Rider's Balance – Understanding the Weight Aids in Pictures*, written by Sylvia Loch. Drawing is by Maggie Raynor. "This is an excellent example of how the rider's weight is pushed onto the outside seat-bone when the rider leans into the canter lead. Weight can be put into the inside leg without leaning when the torso is held upright" (Ref: 7.2).

It is very important for the rider to keep an upright torso. Sometimes riders will tend to lean into the required canter lead. Whilst the inside seat-bone should be slightly weighted, any leaning will actually have the opposite effect – it will push more weight onto the outside seat-bone. This will obviously confuse and hinder the horse.

In Sylvia Loch's brilliant book *The Rider's Balance* (Ref: 7.2), she notes the following:

> There has to be an energy within the rider to initiate the canter strike-off if it is to be upward and instant. We lighten our weight on the back of the saddle to enable the horse to push off the outside hind.

The importance of the inside hip

If the rider loses, or does not have, the advancement of the inside hip, then he is not in the canter position. The canter is a three-beat, skipping movement, bent slightly to the inside. The horse needs to advance the inside hip; therefore, the rider must do the same in order not to hinder the horse's hip. Just try skipping on the ground yourself with your hands on your hips. If your inside hip and inside leg is not in advance, then it is impossible to skip.

As mentioned before, the advancement of the rider's inside hip also has the effect of slightly lightening the outside seat-bone, which facilitates ease of the horse's strike off with the outside hind.

Therefore, the rider's position is crucial in the canter. The rider not being in this canter position is the reason for most incorrect strike offs as well as failure to continue to canter. The re-aligning of the rider's hips and legs to the neutral position is a definite aid to the horse to cease cantering.

If you, as a rider, find it very difficult to put yourself correctly into either right or left canter position, it may be worth considering enlisting the help of a human chiropractor or osteopath. In fact, it is a good idea to have a check-up treatment every so often anyway, in the same way as it is good for the horse.

Where to ask for strike off in the arena

It is generally thought best to request the strike off in a corner of the arena as this will give the horse the best chance of striking off on the correct leading leg. Be careful not to ride too deep into the corner. The first corner of the short side is often used, as if this fails, then another attempt can be made in the next corner. However, this could be off-putting to some horses since the next corner looming in front of them could be frightening. This may depend upon the size of the horse.

Sometimes a pole placed on an oblique angle just off the corner may help the horse to give a correct strike off. Of course, this will only help if the horse is already accustomed to walking and trotting over poles on the ground. If he is not, it is likely to frighten him and make things much worse.

Striking off from trot or walk

Although asking for strike off is normally first done from trot, as this is far easier for the horse than from walk, it is worth bearing in mind that for a small minority of horses, it may actually be easier from walk. It is certainly easier for the rider to place themselves in the canter position correctly at the walk. We must bear in mind that cantering from the walk is normally a fairly advanced exercise and requires a good degree of strength; however, it is possible that if the rider begins to initiate the canter in walk, the horse may go into a couple of slow trot strides, then be able to strike off into canter. This should only be attempted with horses who have attained a good deal of strength, balance and flexibility in the trot. It can be helpful for the small number of horses for whom cantering from the trot is initially far too frightening and they cannot seem to do anything but rush off. Everything should be kept calm and 'matter of fact'. If the strike off doesn't happen, it can always be attempted another day.

Once the canter strike off has been calmly achieved with this method, then it is best to try from a normal trot.

Disunited canter

The canter can become disunited at any time and at any stage of training, whenever the horse becomes suddenly unbalanced for any reason. It may happen perhaps on a corner, when the rider uses too strong an outside leg, or sometimes there appears to be no apparent reason – just a 'glitch'. It can even happen if the horse tries to make a flying change – he may change in front and not behind. His legs are just in a muddle. It can, of course, also happen at the strike off.

To the rider, it will feel uncomfortable and just 'not right'. To the onlooker, it usually looks as though the two back legs are moving together.

Don't panic – just bring the horse gently back to trot as soon as possible, and ask for another correct strike off into canter.

Different types of canter in the dressage arena

There are four types of canter recognised in the dressage arena:

Working canter: As with the working trot, working canter is the natural, basic canter, which the horse will assume of his own accord when asked to canter, provided he is fairly balanced and in rhythm.

Medium canter: In a similar way to the medium trot, medium canter should consist of slightly longer strides, or bounds, somewhere between working and extended canter. It should not consist of faster strides, although obviously, longer strides will cover the ground faster.

Extended canter: This consists of the longest canter strides the horse is able to produce according to his breed, type and conformation. The term is self-explanatory, and the whole frame of the horse is extended but without the weight falling to the forehand, so a degree of collection is still required. It should never be attempted until collection in canter is well established. Sometimes in the show ring, the extended canter may be referred to as 'the gallop'.

Collected canter: This, again, is self-explanatory. The horse should take a considerable amount of weight back onto the haunches. The canter should be relatively slow in advancement and the steps should be higher. There must be no pulling with the reins or hyperflexion of the head and neck. It is a very advanced movement and often takes years to achieve.

I believe that shortening and lengthening in canter is much more difficult than in trot and should never be attempted until a high degree of training has been attained.

References

Ref: 7.1 – 'Dressage for the 21st Century' – Belasik, Paul – J.A. Allen – 2001.
Ref: 7.2 – 'The Rider's Balance – Understanding the Weight Aids in Pictures' – Loch, Sylvia – Kenilworth Press – 2018.

Turns and circles   **8**

Including turn on the forehand, turn on the haunches (demi-pirouette) and serpentines, as well as flexion and straightness in the school

Turns and circles are an intrinsic part of training. The first turns the horse has to negotiate, of course, are the corners of the arena. This should be done in walk and the corners taken wide; it is not a good idea to ride deep into the corners until the horse is fairly well advanced in schooling. It is useful to think of the corner as a quarter of a circle, and the aids should be used accordingly.

Likewise, early circle work should be ridden only on large circles at first in walk.

Seat and weight aids for the turn

The seat and weight aids should be the first aids to be employed, before any rein aids are given.

The weight aids on the turn are most important and helpful, utilising the laws of nature. When the rider makes a slight shift in their weight to one side, it is natural for the horse to follow and move his weight in that direction. This is the most comfortable way for him as it keeps his own balance in line with that of the rider.

DOI: 10.1201/9781003503422-9

A turn to the right

In a turn, say, to the right, the centre of balance will move to the right. The rider should put a little more weight into the right stirrup, and therefore the right seat-bone will be weighted slightly. The leg and seat aids work in unison.

The inside (right) leg should remain at the girth (the on-the-girth position), in contact with the horse but not pushing. This acts as a sort of pillar support for the horse to turn around. The correct 'on the girth' position is actually just behind the girth (see Chapter 13 for photos of a rider's leg positioning).

At the same time, the outside (left) leg is taken back behind the girth slightly. This will have the effect of moving the seat and putting a little more weight on the inside (right) seat-bone, as the right hip will be advanced. This will help with the weighting and lengthening of the right leg. The advancement of the right hip is also important as it will allow the horse's right hip to advance as it needs to in a right turn. All this can be done simultaneously and with very little effort and can soon become second nature.

The amount of weight taken to the inside, and the amount of advancement of the inside hip, will depend upon the degree of bend required. For instance, for a simple turn at the corner of the arena, this will be minimal and momentary. When the turn is complete, then the leg and seat aids return to neutral position.

Here's what Col. Podhajsky says about the importance of the rider's inside leg on the corner (Ref: 8.1):

> The rider's inside leg is of great importance, because it not only has to push the horse forward and prevent the hindquarters from falling in – a fault equally as bad as falling out – but it also has to bend the horse round itself through his whole length and thus maintain a correct position. The rider must be careful when passing through a corner neither to remain behind the motion with the upper part of his body nor to lean forward in the saddle. He should sit slightly to the inside and not allow the weight of his body to be drawn to the outside by the action of his outside leg.

The rider should keep the torso upright and well supported to avoid leaning to the inside or collapsing at the waist, which, as mentioned before, would have the opposite of the required effect, that is, it would put more weight onto the outside seat-bone. The rider's head and shoulders should follow the turn so that the outside shoulder is brought around slightly in advance of the inside shoulder. This should not be exaggerated but should follow the degree of the turn required. In a turn at the corner of the arena, it will again just be momentary. This follows the degree of turn of the horse's shoulder.

Rein aids for the turn

The rein aids work in unison with the seat and leg, but the seat and leg are predominant, and perhaps a fraction of a second precede the rein aids. When the horse has become used to following the weight of the rider and it is second nature for both, then the rein aids can be minimal; in fact, it is quite possible to turn without any reins. However, the gentle support of the rein is definitely a help to the horse.

The frequent practice of turning the horse simply by pulling the inside rein cannot be criticised enough. It generally results in a drastic, unnecessary turn of the head and neck. The amount of bend in the neck should be no more than the bend in the rest of the body. The pull on the inside rein will pull the horse's weight onto the inside shoulder, and he will be forced to make an unbalanced, ungainly turn. Whereas, when the correct aids are used, that is, the seat and weight aids initiating the turn and correct rein aids, the horse will turn utilising the hind legs, bringing the inside hind leg more underneath his body to support the centre of balance. This is the whole point of work on the turns and circles; it strengthens the hind legs and helps the horse to support the weight with the hindquarters instead of the vulnerable front legs.

The correct rein aids for the turn are for the rider to indicate the flexion to the inside with a gentle squeeze of the inside rein and possibly a gentle give and take with this rein if required. But, very importantly, this should be backed up by the outside rein being held gently but decisively on the neck so as to support the outside shoulder and prevent any falling onto the inside foreleg. This supporting rein should never be pulled backwards but held on the neck. As the horse turns his head and neck in the turn, this outside rein will automatically be 'filled' by the turn in the neck, and the feel in the rider's outside hand will become a little firmer, but it should never deteriorate into a pull and should not be exaggerated. Enough 'give' in this rein has to be allowed to enable the horse to make the turn.

Here's another quote from Col. Alois Podhajsky in his book *The Complete Training of Horse and Rider* (Ref: 8.1): "If the outside rein is not applied (in

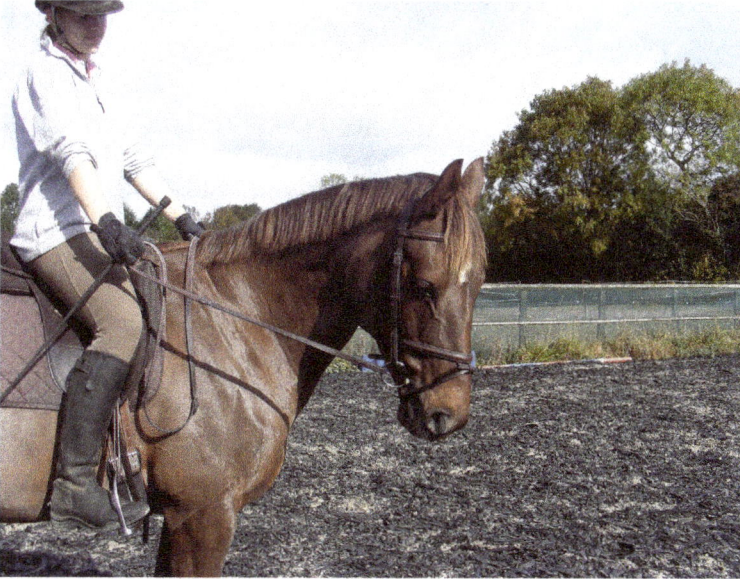

Figure 8.1 Correct Open Rein

This is the correct open rein aid. The hand is taken out to the side and not back. The horse is not pulled out of balance, and the head and neck is not unduly flexed. Photo by Anne Wilson.

the turn) the horse will not execute a turn but follow the action of the inside rein by bending only his neck".

An open rein aid

For a totally untrained, recently backed horse, the use of an open rein aid may be employed to make it clear to him what is desired, that is, that he should turn his head and neck in that direction. In this case, the rein is taken out to the side in the direction of the turn. The outside rein should still be held in contact, and the open rein should not be taken so far as to cause too much bend in the neck. This rein should definitely never be taken backwards, just gently to the inside.

Keeping the hands level

It is important that the hands should be held fairly low and level at the withers. Many riders have a tendency, especially when separating the hands,

Figure 8.2 Incorrect Open Rein
This horse is being pulled completely out of balance with a large amount of weight falling onto the forehand. Photo by Lesley Skipper.

as in the open rein aid, to lower the inside hand. This is not good for the horse as it alters the action of the bit, causing it to be unlevel in the mouth.

Once the horse is more accustomed to the aids for turning, the open rein should be ceased. It is better to use the hands together as soon as the horse understands what is required.

Uses of circle work

Although forward and straight is the first exercise for the ridden horse, as established, work on the circle is essential in the training of any horse, no matter which discipline he is destined to follow. When the horse is bent correctly on the bend, he is 'straight' in dressage terms. Here are some of the benefits:

1. Circling exercises and strengthens the inside hind leg. When ridden correctly, circling is the first exercise to help the horse to take more weight in the hindquarters and thereby lighten the forehand by reaching 'through', that is, forward and further underneath the belly towards the centre of balance.
2. Circling makes the horse more flexible and balanced.
3. Circling should, of course, be practised equally on both reins. In this way, it helps to make the horse more ambidextrous and to minimise the 'stiff' side.

Misuses of circle work

Excessive use of circle work is common, as is riding too small a circle too soon in the training. These two mistakes can be very damaging to the horse's joints, tendons, ligaments and muscles. The smaller the circle, the more strenuous it is for the horse. The larger the horse, the more strain the circle will cause. This must be borne in mind, and the larger horse be worked on a larger circle.

Circle work is good for strengthening and suppling, but when overdone, it causes strain. The aim in all classical training is to strengthen without strain.

We should build up the work on the circle slowly, first by riding large circles in walk and not progressing to trot until the horse is fairly well muscled.

We can, when the horse is strong enough, progress to smaller circles, say 15 or even 10 metres, but definitely not in trot until later in training.

Even when the horse is very fit and strong, there must be nothing more boring and disheartening (for horse and rider alike) than constant trotting in circles. The work should always be in moderation and interspersed with other exercises, involving going large with lots of turns and changes of rein. There are a multitude of ways we can make schooling interesting and variable to keep both horse and rider engrossed.

The other big mistake so often made is that of rushing, or going too fast on the circle in all three gaits. There is no need for speed, and it is detrimental. Circling is beneficial as long as there is reasonable impulsion, flexion of the joints and the desire to move forward.

Common rider mistakes on the circle

As previously discussed, most people and horses are one sided. In the case of humans, we are normally right-handed (and right-sided), so both our right hands and legs are stronger and more dominant than the left. It is easy for the rider to overuse the right rein (or left if left-handed) and cause too much bend in the neck. Also, if the right leg is applied too heavily, it will push the horse outwards, and if not allowed to move out by the outside rein, he will overbend the body and be unbalanced.

Some riders who are very right-handed may inadvertently use too much right rein on a left circle, which will prevent the correct bend to the left.

The inside leg is important on a circle as a pillar for support; this should be just a gentle presence on the horse's side but can be used a little more against the horse to send him out on the circle, if this is what is required, or to prevent him from falling in.

Obviously, everything I have said about right-sidedness can be reversed if the rider is left-sided.

All these intricacies are a matter of feel, and the slightest adjustments (or misalignments) can make a big difference. It is really helpful to have an experienced and knowledgeable classical trainer on the ground to help in this regard.

Making a deeper angled turn

Most of what I have said about circle work can be applied to making an angled turn.

The sharper the turn required, the more rider weight should be taken in the direction of the turn and the more the inside hip should advance.

The support of the outside rein is imperative in an angled turn; it will assist the turn and prevent the horse from falling onto the inside shoulder, but it should not be so tight as to prevent the horse from turning. As always, no pulling on the reins should ever occur.

More advanced turns and circles

Turn on the forehand and turn on the haunches (or demi-pirouette)

Turn on the forehand and turn on the hocks or haunches are often thought of as similar types of movements, and in some ways, they are. However, it is important to understand the differences not only in how they are implemented but also in their purpose and effects upon the horse.

Turn on the forehand, as well as turn on the hocks from a standstill, are definitely not classical exercises. All classical exercises are designed to help the horse build up correctly towards the final goal, that is, to improve strength and flexibility of the joints and tendons in order to take weight back onto the hind legs, thus leading to collection.

Turn on the forehand tends to have the opposite effect in that it encourages weight onto the forehand – the exact opposite of our main aim. However, it can be a very useful movement to teach the horse to move away from a unilateral leg aid of the rider, whilst being supported by outside aids of leg and hand. It can be invaluable at times when out hacking in order to open gates or perform other tasks. Once taught, it should only be practised occasionally so as not to encourage weight transference to the forehand.

Turn on the hocks from a standstill also does not help the horse in the quest for weight transference to the hindquarters. It may not have the opposite effect as does turn on the forehand, but it is of no use in the quest for collection. Turn on the hocks can also be a very useful, practical movement for, say, moving away from an obstruction or maybe moving around a gate.

Therefore, as noted, turn on the forehand and turn on the hocks from a standstill are both manoeuvres and not exercises.

Of course, turn on the hocks in motion is totally different and is a beneficial exercise.

The turn on the haunches or pirouette is definitely a classical exercise

Turn on the hocks when ridden at the walk or trot (otherwise referred to as the pirouette), is a very useful classical exercise which builds up strength and flexibility of the inside hind leg and strengthens the back and quarter muscles. The key differentiating element here is that the rhythm of the gait is not interrupted, causing the horse to step well under his body mass with the inside hind leg.

The aim and aids for turn on the forehand

The aim is to ask the horse to turn his quarters around a given inside foreleg without any forward or backward steps. It is always carried out from the halt, and on completion, be it one or two steps or a complete 360-degree

turn, the horse should be ridden immediately forward. The final aim is usually a 180-degree turn, that is, a turnabout or change of rein.

How to ride a turn on the forehand around the right foreleg

Halt the horse two or three metres in from the track and parallel to it.
This helps to keep the horse straight. The aim is for the horse to lift his
right foreleg up and down, more or less on the same spot, whilst taking his
quarters to the left.

A slight flexion to the right

The horse is asked to flex slightly to the right. All that is required for this
flexion is a slight bend in the head and neck, just enough for the rider to
see a glimpse of the horse's right eye.

**The rider's right leg behind the girth nudges the quarters
away to the left**

The rider's left leg is kept on the girth ready to be gently but firmly applied
if the horse should start to move the forehand away to the left. Then the
rider's right leg is placed behind the girth and gently asks for the quarters
to move to the left. This is best done by means of a series of nudges of
the rider's leg. Each time the horse's quarters step away from the leg,
the rider ceases this nudging aid as an indication to the horse that he has
done as required. If another step is required the leg gently nudges once
more and so on. I suggest that two steps would be ample for both horse
and rider in the early stages.

Rein aids during turn on the forehand

During these leg aids, the hands support the horse. The right rein does very
little except to ask for slight right flexion by a gentle squeezing action on the
rein, which is immediately ceased when the horse responds. The left rein is
the important rein to indicate to the horse that he should not step forwards,
but it should never be a pulling action, merely restraining. If the horse does
misunderstand and starts to move forward, just calmly ride him forwards
and come to a halt again to make another attempt.

   If the horse appears confused at first, then it may help to halt in front
of a fence or gate, in this way making it clear to the horse that forward
movement is not required. Also, a helper on the ground can show the

horse what is wanted by gently encouraging the quarters in the required direction.

It should go without saying that the horse should never be forced or agitated by this movement; begin with just one or two steps, then enlarge upon it another day. Never make many attempts during one schooling session. If things go wrong, there's always another day.

I am of the firm opinion that, although the turn on the forehand may be good in the very early stages of training to teach the horse to move away from the unilateral leg aid, its use should be confined to this, or practical use, and it should not be used on an on-going basis in training. If this movement is never taught, it will do no harm, as quarter- and demi-pirouettes are so much more beneficial and important.

The aim for quarter-turn on the haunches or quarter-pirouette in walk

The aim of the quarter-pirouette (which is the same thing as a quarter-turn on the haunches) is for the horse to make a turn more from the hocks and to bring his forehand around with the hint of a right-angled turn. The outside hind leg describes part of a small circle. It is important not to restrain the horse too much with the outside rein (although he definitely does need plenty of support from this rein) so that the rhythm of the walk is not interfered with, or to cause the horse to either pivot on the inside hind foot or move it up and down on the spot (as he is required to do with the inside forefoot in the turn on the forehand). No crossing over of legs is required in the pirouette; this is considered a fault and means that the forward rhythm of the gait has been interfered with. Each foot should make a definite independent track as in the four beat rhythm of the walk.

A good rhythmic walk on the track will prepare the horse, and a light half-halt a stride or two beforehand is sometimes helpful, just to rebalance him and warn him of something different to come.

It is only sensible to teach this exercise from the track where you have the fence or wall to prevent the quarters from swinging outwards. If no arena is available, then a flat field with a fence or hedge can be made use of. If you have the benefit of an arena, it is best to choose to begin the exercise adjacent to say the letter 'E' so you have a good visual aid to help you straighten the horse after the turn and ride straight towards 'B' (see Figure 8.3).

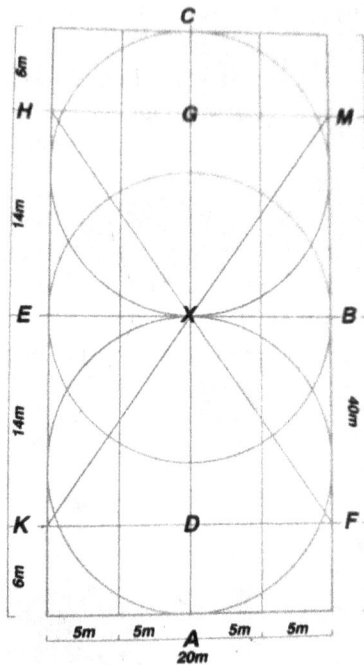

Figure 8.3 A 20 × 40-Metre Arena

The dressage letters and markings show where three 20-metre circles can be ridden with guidance from the markers, centre and quarter lines. Also, where to change the rein across the diagonal.

The rider's aids for the quarter-turn on the haunches or quarter-pirouette in walk

On the right rein, having given a gentle warning half-halt after 'K', the rider should feel the right rein just before 'E'. This should only consist of an opening and closing of the fingers of the right hand. On no account should the right rein take or overbend the horse's neck to the right as in an 'open rein aid'. To do so would make it virtually impossible for the horse to perform the turn as required.

After creating this very soft right flexion, the rider's right leg must remain at the girth for support. It is the pillar that the horse is required to turn around and, in this instance, is of utmost importance. The right leg must not push, but it must support.

The rider's upper body

The rider's upper body should be very tall and upright, being very careful not to lean inwards nor to collapse the inside hip.

Weight to the inside

Still in this upright position, the rider should lengthen the inside (right) leg. In other words, put a little more weight into the right stirrup.

The outside leg asks the forehand to move away from the track

At the same time, the rider's outside (left) leg asks the horse's forehand to move away to the right. The left leg (initially near the girth to nudge the forehand across) should slide back as a control to stop the horse's quarters from falling outwards (to the left) as the turn progresses. To instigate the movement of the horse's outside shoulder in a right-hand direction, it is important that the rider uses the whole of their outside (left) leg – the upper thigh is important in this movement.

Upper body and hips turn together

At the same moment as the rider's legs ask for the turn, the rider's upper body and hips turn together in unison. The hands stay together as a pair and turn to the right, together with the shoulders. The rider's hips make a definite turn to the right. The rider's head is obviously turned with the shoulders in unison, and the rider looks where he wants the horse to look.

The outside hand should be firm and supportive

Whilst the rider's inside (right) hand should be soft and giving, encouraging the turn but without pulling or moving to the right, the outside (left) hand must stay firm and supportive against the horse's neck. Provided that the reins are short enough, without pulling at the horse, there should be no need to shorten the outside (left) rein or to pull back with this hand. (Pulling back is always a derogatory step and in this case might change the flexion.) The bend of the horse's head and neck to the right, together with the movement of the shoulders, should be enough to fill this outside rein. The bend, of course, should not be too great.

After completing this quarter-turn at say 'E', as described earlier, the aids should return to neutral and the horse should be straightened and ridden across the school directly to the opposite track at approximately 'B'.

When ridden as described here, the rider should have a good feel of how the horse will mirror the rider. When the rider turns their head, shoulders and upper torso in the direction of the turn and takes the hands in that direction as a pair, accompanied by the other aids, discretely applied (including the weight aid to the inside), the rider will gain a wonderful feeling of oneness with the horse – the horse following the rider's movement without any harsh aids.

The demi-pirouette

When the horse is ready, that is, well established in the quarter-pirouette, then the aids can be continued until a 180-degree turn has been reached. Do not expect the horse to complete the turn in the same spot he started – that is not the purpose. It is better to think of it as part of a very small circle so that the rhythm of the gait is not interrupted and there is no pivoting on the inside leg, nor crossing of legs.

A quarter-pirouette in trot

The aids as described earlier are the same for a quarter-pirouette in trot, but obviously, you must not expect such a sharp degree in the turn; there should still be a feeling of turning from the hocks. Do not begin this in trot until the horse is well advanced in training.

As in all exercises, pirouettes should not be over-ridden, especially when first introduced.

I hope that this clears up many of the misconceptions of these movements/exercises and explains their various applications and purposes.

Serpentines

A serpentine is a series of loops ridden across the arena. In a 20 × 40 m arena (see Figure 8.3), the most usual serpentine is that of three loops. Some people do ride four- or even five-looped serpentines, but this is normally in a 20 × 60 m arena. Obviously, more loops are more demanding, so three loops will suffice to begin with.

The serpentine is a very good exercise; it introduces variety into the schooling session and should be ridden by commencing on each rein equally. But, as in all things, it is best not to overdo it; two or four serpentines in one schooling session is enough.

At first, the serpentine should be ridden in walk, and later in trot. It facilitates the flexibility and balance of the horse and, when well ridden, consolidates responsiveness to the rider's aids.

It is very demanding on the rider as each turn to and from the track is ridden as a bend, or as part of a circle. The rider needs to change the aids (weight, body, etc.) frequently and smoothly when negotiating each change of bend. This takes a lot of co-ordination because if the rider is a fraction of a second out-of-time, this will throw the horse out of balance. For this reason, it is best to practise serpentines many times in walk, possibly for several weeks, before attempting it in trot.

The aids for a three-looped serpentine, commencing on the right rein

To ride a three-looped serpentine, enter the school at 'A', ride straight down the centre line to 'C' and turn right. The horse should be flexed, or bent, slightly to the right. Keep your right leg at the girth as a support to the horse, especially approaching the corner, where you will bend right. Keep this right bend and shortly after passing 'M' (the quarter marker), leave the track and head towards the opposite side of the school. Initiate the turn with the outside (left) leg behind the girth together with a very slight 'step' into the right stirrup, encouraging the horse to turn right. Your outside (left) leg is behind the girth on the turn to discourage any outward swing of the quarters. Your inside (right) leg is on the girth to support and give any necessary encouraging impulsion aid. Your outside (left) rein is held to support the outside shoulder but should not impede the turn. Your inside rein suggests the turn but does not pull the head around. Your upper body remains very erect and turns with the horse, shoulder to shoulder, and hip to hip. Your head turns with the horse's head, and your eyes look where you want your horse to look.

On completion of the turn to the right, and before passing over the centre line (that is, the invisible line between 'A' and 'C'), return your aids to neutral, straighten the horse, and look towards the opposite side of the school.

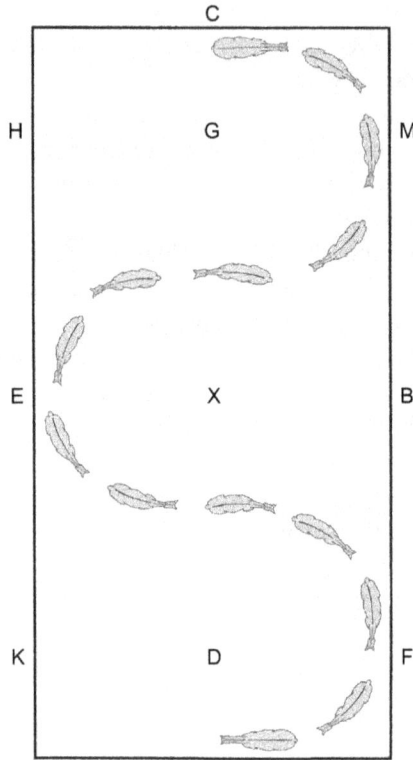

Figure 8.4 A Serpentine

This is a conventional three-looped serpentine, using part of a circle to make the turn. Figure courtesy of Lesley Skipper.

On passing through the centre of the school, you need to prepare for a left bend when reaching the opposite track of the school. All the above aids are reversed for the left bend.

As you will see from the diagram, this process is carried out three times throughout this serpentine. You will therefore have made two turns to the right and one to the left. When you ride the serpentine commencing on the left rein, you will make two left bending turns and one right.

Riding the serpentine using quarter-turns

As a much more demanding exercise, you can ride the serpentine utilising quarter-turns, as in the quarter-pirouette. You should ride the first part of

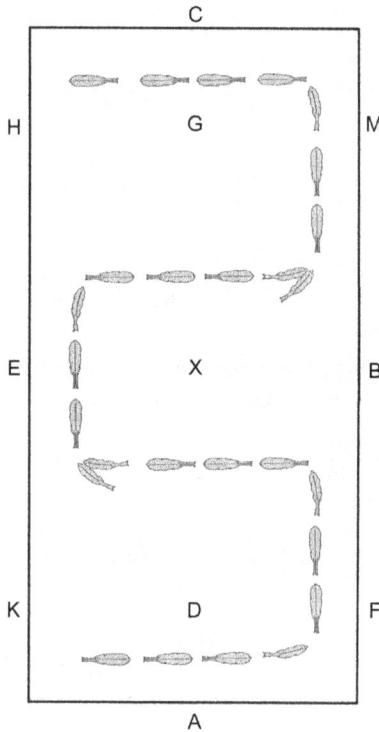

Figure 8.5 A Serpentine Using Quarter-Turns

This figure shows the three-looped serpentine using quarter-turns (quarter-pirouettes). Note the angled turn of the pirouette is only used when turning away from the track. Figure courtesy of Lesley Skipper.

the turn on approach to the track as a normal bending turn, then ask for a more acute angled turn as you turn away from the track. The same aids are used as described for quarter-turn on the haunches.

Don't be surprised if you do not achieve too much in the way of a turn on the haunches to begin with, but given time, you will feel the difference. Be patient, and be pleased when the horse is listening to you, even if he cannot quite comply to begin with.

Flexion and straightness in the school

As mentioned previously, the horse is straight in dressage terms when he can bend correctly (his body aligned to the bend) and evenly on a curve or bend in either direction.

There are very few times in the school when the horse should be dead straight, that is, without flexion in either direction. These are when being ridden straight down the centre line, changing the rein across the diagonal, or crossing straight from one side of the track to the other. This includes crossing the centre of the school during a serpentine.

At all other times when moving around the track of the school (once the horse is beyond the very early stages of being ridden), he should have a slight flexion in the head and neck to the inside, even when travelling straight down the long side of the school. For instance, when riding down the long side on the left rein, the rider should just about be able to see the horse's left eye (without leaning down or bending their own head) in readiness to make a left turn at the corner of the school. If the horse has a full, long mane, this may hide the eye, so a knowledgeable person on the ground should be able to advise in this regard.

Reference

Ref: 8.1 – 'The Complete Training of Horse and Rider' – Podhajsky, Col. Alois – Translated by Eva Podhajsky & Col. V.D.S. Williams – Harrap – 1967.

Introducing lateral exercises

9

Leg-yield, shoulder-fore and shoulder-in

On a very basic level, the young horse should have been prepared for moving laterally whilst being handled on the ground, for instance, moving over sideways when asked, from light pressure or a gentle tap from the rider's hand or whip. The difference now is that we will ask him to move forward and sideways at the same time, whilst carrying the rider, which can seem very different.

I have emphasised previously the need for the horse to be completely at ease with the use of the whip. He should see it as a friendly aid, not as a punishment.

Leg-yield

The first lateral movement normally taught to the horse is leg-yield, which consists of the horse moving forward and sideways, slightly flexed to the inside, away from the direction of the lateral travel, with the forehand preceding the quarters by about half a stride.

Leg-yield is not at all essential; one can begin lateral education with shoulder-fore (the precursor to shoulder-in but with less displacement from the track). Not all trainers use leg-yield because it is not strictly speaking a classical exercise. This is because it does not have the benefits of the classical exercises in that it does not require nor assist in the process of taking weight from the forehand to the quarters, and it does not require actual bend, merely a slight flexion at the head and neck. However, it is very helpful in improving the horse's balance and flexibility as well as teaching him to

DOI: 10.1201/9781003503422-10

move away from the unilateral leg aid of the rider, giving the first glimpse of forward and sideways movement.

Later on in training, leg-yield can be ridden with actual bend, and in this way, it can become more akin to, although not the same as, shoulder-in.

Some people strongly disapprove of leg-yield, taking the view that it is teaching the horse to move forward and sideways across the school in the same way as half-pass except with the bend in the opposite direction, and this can be thought to confuse the horse. I have never found this to be the case. The change in bend makes it a totally different movement, and I find that horses understand it very well, so much so, that later in training, they can move back and forth from leg-yield to half-pass up the centre of the school with ease – each change of bend being effortless. It introduces yet another facet of interest in the school movements, making schooling even more fascinating to horse and rider.

In the beginning, the best way to introduce lateral movements is from the ground with the horse in hand. This can be done for leg-yield as well as shoulder-in.

I strongly disapprove of the type of in-hand work whereby the horse is spun round too fast and on the spot. The aim should be for everything to be done at a steady, relaxed pace with forward momentum taking precedence over the sideways movement.

Leg-yield in hand

The help of a schooling whip is of benefit; as you lead the horse at his head, gently bend him towards you, and as you walk forwards and sideways, just encourage him to move his body in the required direction by holding your hand or whip on his side where your leg would normally be if in the saddle. Remember that in leg-yield, the forehand should be slightly in advance of the quarters. So don't try to make him move laterally with the forehand and quarters on the same track as this would be far too difficult and you would actually lose the benefit of the exercise.

If he seems confused and doesn't allow his quarters to follow, then a gentle touch with the whip on the quarters will show him what is required. But be careful, as this is a balancing act; you want his quarters to follow but not to catch up with the forehand.

Leg-yield under saddle

Leg-yield, like most exercises, should only be practised in walk when first introducing the movement. Leg-yield under saddle may seem quite

Figure 9.1 Leg-Yield
Secret and I, performing simple leg-yield in walk across the school. Photo by Lesley Skipper.

confusing to the horse at first, and he will need to adjust his balance considerably when carrying the rider at the same time, so be patient. You need to be firm with your aids, in order for him to understand, but at the same time the aids should not be harsh nor sporadic. It can be very useful to have a helper on the ground at first, to walk by the horse's shoulder to give a helping hand on his shoulder or girth area just to reinforce your aids and to show more distinctly what is required.

How to approach your first leg-yield

(These instructions are assuming you are using a 20 × 40 metre schooling area.)

The best way to begin is to ride a 20-metre circle, say, on the left rein at the 'A' end of the school. After completing the circle, turn left off the track at the quarter line after 'A'. You will then be aiming to ride forward and sideways towards the track, reaching the track somewhere near the centre marker 'B'.

To make things really easy in the beginning, it is usually a good idea to stay on the short side a little longer after 'A' and turn off nearer to the long side of the track. In this way, you will only have a very short distance to leg-yield before reaching the track. You can gradually increase the distance by turning off the short side earlier until you can eventually turn down the centre line at 'A' and leg-yield halfway across the school, reaching the track between 'B' and 'M'.

Whilst most other exercises can be ridden in the field on a flat piece of ground, providing the ground is neither too hard nor too muddy, it is of great advantage to have a purpose-built arena with a good surface, especially when it comes to lateral work. If this is not possible, then a suitable piece of ground which is fenced in or pegged out, and the use of the usual dressage markers, will be very beneficial.

The aids for leg-yield on the left rein

When you have ridden your circle, you should have established a bend (in this case to the left); as you turn off the track just after 'A' on the left rein, you should endeavour to keep a little left bend. Although bend is not strictly required for leg-yield, an inside flexion is essential. If you start off the exercise with bend and then lose it, so long as the left flexion is still there, things should go well.

If the horse is able to keep the left bend, then all well and good. In this case, your leg-yield will be more akin to a shoulder-in and will be a great preparation for that exercise.

When you turn off the track after 'A' (as described earlier), slide your right (outside) leg slightly back from the hip. This is to include your thigh, not just the lower leg, being careful not to lift your heel. This outside leg should be in place but passive. It is there to prevent the quarters from swinging out towards the right, so pressure should only be placed on the horse with this leg if this should happen. But it is important that the horse feels that the leg is there.

At the same time as moving your outside leg back, make pressure aids with the inside leg on the girth. This can be in the form of a pushing movement or a series of gentle taps, whichever the horse responds to and finds easiest to understand. Sometimes merely a very slight weight against the horse's side is enough for him to move sideways away from the pressure.

It is of great advantage if you minutely weight your right stirrup (and therefore your right seat-bone). This is actually difficult whilst your right leg is taken back. The well-balanced horse will automatically move in the direction of your weight in order to stay in balance with the rider. It is an instinctive reaction and a law of nature. In all but very exceptional circumstances, the horse will move towards the weight. This should be borne in mind in all our riding.

Keep your hands low and as quiet as possible, but do not throw away the reins. Keep the right (outside) rein on the horse's neck with a firm, yet gentle, supportive feel. The left (inside) rein should be kept as quiet as possible but can suggest the retention of the left flexion, if necessary, by 'feeling' fingers on the rein as though gently squeezing water from a sponge.

Although it is important that the forehand should precede the quarters, it is imperative that it should not precede too much, otherwise the horse will be walking straight to the track on an oblique line without making any sideways steps.

The right (outside) rein on the horse's neck is very important to the horse in this respect. A slight increase in pressure on the outside rein will facilitate more sideways movement and bring the forehand to the required alignment. This definitely does not mean a harsh rein aid but a feeling, firm and supportive one, which needs to be against the horse's neck. Be careful not to let your right hand come over the withers to the left-hand side. This could happen if your reins are too long, so make sure they are short enough for you to keep the constant, sympathetic contact with the horse's mouth. Longer reins usually cause a less consistent, jabbing contact, which is not appreciated by the horse at all. You can be much kinder and more accurate with short reins.

Whilst practising this exercise, you will see how a minute amount of extra feel on the outside rein will have an arresting effect on the forward movement, causing more sideways steps. Obviously, you don't want to overdo this; it's a matter of finding the correct balance. As a general rule of thumb, forward progression should always take precedence over lateral steps.

If you and your horse find it difficult to move the forehand over before the quarters, try asking for the sideways movement immediately as the forehand has left the track, with the quarters still on the track. Quite often leg-yield is very hard to establish if your horse is straight before you start. Of course, as he becomes more au fait with the movement, this will be no problem.

Obviously, the aids described here should be reversed when riding the exercise on the opposite rein – on the right rein towards the left.

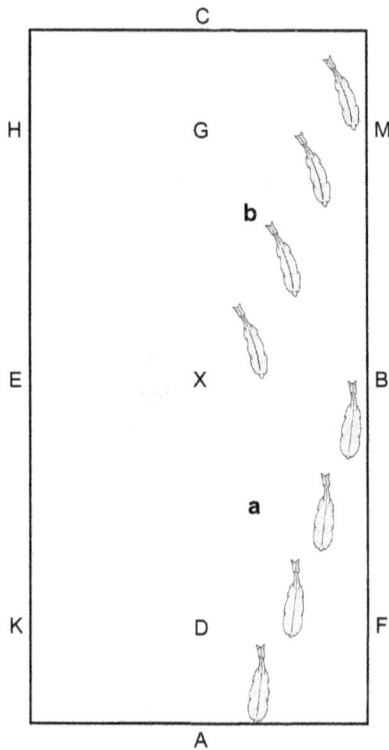

Figure 9.2 Leg-Yield and Shoulder-In Across School

This figure shows (a) leg-yield across school and (b) shoulder-in across school.

You can clearly see the similarity in the movement but the difference in the bend and angle of the shoulder. Figure courtesy of Lesley Skipper.

Body posture

It is important to have a good classical position: upright with expanded chest. A common mistake is one of trying too hard to push the horse sideways with the inside leg, which often results in collapsing the hip. This is much less likely to happen if the rider thinks 'up and tall' at all times.

Leg-yield can also usefully be used when spiralling in and out of circles. This is a very good exercise. It is also extremely important when out hacking in manoeuvring past parked vehicles.

Leg-yield up the track

Leg-yield up the track is not something I would recommend; in fact, I actively discourage it. However, many trainers use this movement to teach

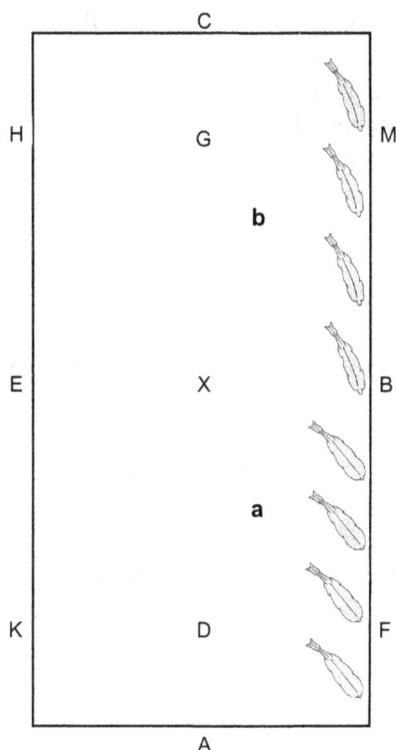

Figure 9.3 Straight Leg-Yield Up Track and Shoulder-In Up Track

This figure shows (a) straight leg-yield up track and (b) shoulder-in up track.

You can clearly see the similarity of the movements but the straight body of the leg-yield, with slightly more displacement of the shoulder from the track, as opposed to the bend of the shoulder-in. This, I find, can be confusing to the horse. Diagram courtesy of Lesley Skipper.

the horse to yield to the leg, and to that extent, I suppose it does its job, but I don't think it has any other useful purpose and can be derogatory.

I disapprove of the movement because it is much more difficult than the simple forward moving leg-yield described previously since the horse is moving sideways with no forward progression. It places the horse in the general position of shoulder-in but without the necessary bend and preparatory strengthening which he needs in order to bring his inside hind leg forward and under the body mass. Therefore, there is no weight transference onto the haunches, and it does not aid collection.

If the horse is positioned with his quarters on the track and forehand taken in at a similar angle to the track as shoulder-in, but not encouraged to bend but merely to travel up the track in a lateral movement with a more or less straight body, then this is a leg-yield. I think that once this movement is taught to the horse deliberately (it will happen when first teaching shoulder-in anyway), then it must be confusing to the horse if he has been praised for this and thinks this is correct to be later told, 'well actually, no that's not right, you must now bend'. If you are going to teach shoulder-in, I believe it is far better to encourage a uniform bend from head to tail throughout the body to begin with, even if it takes some time to perfect. One can have patience, and it is far better than teaching him the wrong thing in the first place.

The benefits of simple leg-yield with flexion or bend

The simple leg-yield across the diagonal, as described earlier, is far easier for the newcomer to learn to move forward and sideways, and it is a good preparation for shoulder-in since it teaches the horse to move away from the direction of bend/flexion from the rider's inside leg. It also assists the horse's flexibility and balance, which the straight leg-yield does not.

One note of interest: in all classical lateral exercises, except for shoulder-in, the horse moves towards the bend, away from the rider's outside leg and into the supportive inside leg. Shoulder-in is the only one where he moves away from the bend.

Shoulder-In

Francois Robichon de la Guérinière, in his book *School of Horsemanship*, notes the following (Ref: 9.1):

> This exercise (the shoulder-in) has so many benefits that I regard it as the alpha and omega of all exercises for the horse which are intended to develop complete suppleness and perfect agility in all its parts.

Shoulder-in is undoubtedly the most important exercise we teach our horses. If your horse never progresses any further but has mastered the shoulder-in correctly and evenly on both reins, he will be lighter in hand, more balanced and have a much better chance of staying sound well into old age.

If you are adept at work in hand, it is quite permissible to begin a few steps of shoulder-in while walking in hand at a fairly early stage of training; this can be very helpful. That said, I always think that the real work starts here under saddle but not until the horse is reasonably strong, supple and advanced enough.

It is probably the most talked of and written about exercise. There are more differing opinions about the refinements and details of this exercise than any other, but, in classical circles, it is generally agreed that Francois Robichon de la Guérinière was the innovator of the shoulder-fore and shoulder-in, and he did refine it into the exercise we know today. However, there were other great riding masters before him who laid down many of the basic principles, notably, the Englishman William Cavendish, Duke of Newcastle.

However, the great difference was brought about when Guérinière realised the benefit of riding shoulder-in down the track of the school. The quarters were then contained by the wall of the school and more emphasis was put upon the hindquarters; thus, the shoulders were lightened like never before. That is why it is such an important, beneficial exercise.

Guérinière designed shoulder-in as a four-track movement, whereas in today's FEI competition rules, it is defined as a three-track exercise.

Shoulder-fore

To begin with, we are only going to ask for shoulder-fore, which is merely shoulder-in at a shallower angle. The preparation and aids are exactly the

Figure 9.4 Shoulder-fore

Here is my mare Secret in shoulder-fore in fairly early training. She is approaching the shoulder-in position but not quite. As you can see, the inside hind is not going to be 'stepping through' as much as in the shoulder-in. Photo by Lesley Skipper.

same as for shoulder-in; the difference is that the shoulder is taken in at a smaller angle to that of shoulder-in. From here-on-in, when I refer to shoulder-in, the same will apply to shoulder-fore.

Preparation for shoulder-in

You can do a lot to prepare for shoulder-in by gradually increasing the amount of bend when you practise leg-yield. Although leg-yield does not require bend but merely a flexion away from the direction of movement, when performed as we see in Figure 9.1, it does become much more like the movement of shoulder-in. Even so, they are not exactly the same, and leg-yield is easier.

Where to practise the first steps of shoulder-in

In the beginning of training, shoulder-in should always be practised on the track. It is best to start after a corner. It is, in my opinion, foolhardy to attempt it anywhere else in the school at this stage.

Once shoulder-in becomes easy both in walk and trot on the track, then you can use it anywhere in the school, say down the centre line or on the circle.

Shoulder-in on the circle

Shoulder-in on the circle does not have the same benefits as when it is ridden on the track, but it is still beneficial and introduces variety to the schooling.

The reason it is not usually as beneficial is that it is extremely hard to maintain the correct bend and to prevent the quarters from moving outwards, which the wall of the arena will naturally do when ridden on the track. The shoulders are lightened when the quarters are contained.

Shoulder-out

Shoulder-out is merely shoulder-in performed from a different position – a mirror image of shoulder-in. When ridden, say, down the long side of the arena, the horse obviously needs to be brought to the inside of the track in order to make room for the shoulder to be taken out. When ridden on the circle, it can be very difficult to maintain the circle.

Figure 9.5 Three-Track Shoulder-In

This is a good three-track shoulder-in (although my torso could be more supportive). The horse is moving away from the direction of the bend. Photo by Lesley Skipper.

The footfalls of the three-track shoulder-in

This will involve a displacement of the shoulders from the track of about 30 degrees:

1st footprint – outside hind
2nd footprint – the inside hind will step into the track of the outside fore
3rd footprint – inside fore

The footfalls of the four-track shoulder-in

This involves a displacement of the shoulders from the track of about 40 degrees, in which case each foot will make its own track.

The horse's body movements in shoulder-in

To perform a three-track shoulder-in, which is normally required in competition, the horse should move sideways down the track with the hind legs on the track and forehand taken inwards, away from the track at an angle of roughly 30 degrees (less for shoulder-fore, which is advised when first teaching the exercise).

The horse should be bent away from the direction of travel with equal bend from poll to tail. So, on the left rein, the horse should be bent to the left and travelling down the track to the right.

There should be no excessive bend in the head and neck; this is a common fault at the beginning of training.

The inside hind leg (in left rein shoulder-in, this is the left hind) does most of the extra work in that it comes forward, moves in front of the outside one to underneath the belly, steps into the print of the outside fore – thus creating three tracks – and pushes the horse sideways up the track.

A four-track shoulder-in

This is a more advanced movement and requires a larger displacement from the track – about 40 degrees. If the horse does not bend correctly, he will take less weight back onto his haunches, and this is more likely at this angle, in which case the exercise is rendered far less beneficial.

I would certainly not worry about how many tracks my horse is making with his feet. Just concentrate on good bending, a definite displacement of the shoulder from the track (even if a shallow angle) and sideways progression.

The misleading four-track shoulder-in

Obviously, the greater the angle from the track, the greater the bend from poll to tail should be, and herein lies the difficulty with the four-track shoulder-in.

A good shoulder-in at this angle requires greater suppleness and strength in the hind legs, and it can only really be executed correctly by a fairly advanced horse. However, when a strong, supple, well-prepared horse is able to perform this exercise on four tracks correctly, then I believe it should be ridden in this way as Guérinière intended.

Many horses offer to bring their shoulders in from the track at a greater angle than expected in order to straighten their body, which is in fact easier to do at this angle. This obviously makes it much easier for them, and the unsuspecting, fairly inexperienced rider is overjoyed with this offering, failing to realise that they have lost the bend. This renders the exercise no

Figure 9.6 Four-Track Shoulder-In

This is a good four-track shoulder-in. Note the greater angle from the track and greater bend in the horse's body. The horse is moving away from the direction of the bend. Photo by Lesley Skipper.

more than a leg-yield up the track, losing the physical benefits of weight transference to the haunches and lightening of the forehand. This is why I am definitely not a fan of teaching leg-yield up the track because, in essence, it is teaching the horse something which is wrong.

The rider's aids for shoulder-in (and shoulder-fore)

It is best to prepare for shoulder-in by riding a fairly small circle, say, on the right rein. Ride your circle in the corner of the school just before the long side.

You should already have your outside leg back and inside leg on the girth with your right hip in advance of the left.

Keeping the right bend, when you have ridden one circle, just as the horse steps off the track with his forelegs and is about to begin another circle, you ask him to step sideways away from your right leg, into your left rein.

Your shoulders should be turned inwards at the angle to which you want your horse's shoulders. Don't forget to turn your head with your shoulders and look where you want your horse to look – not up the track!

Keeping your hands together, take both hands to the right with your shoulders as they turn. The outside (left rein) should be on the neck, but don't take your left hand across the withers to the right, just keep it at the withers.

Your left (outside) leg should be back, not just from the knee but from the thigh. This leg should normally be quietly laid on the horse and only brought into play, if necessary, should the quarters begin to swing outwards.

The horse is bent around your right leg, which gently but decisively asks the horse to move away and sideways up the track, either by a gentle pushing or tapping movement, whichever the horse responds to best and whichever you have used previously when asking for leg-yield.

The importance of the outside rein

The main thing which tells the horse not to walk forward onto a circle or diagonally across the school is the supportive and firm outside rein on the neck. If you have taken both hands to the right and the horse is bent to the right, then this should be enough to give the left rein the extra tension required as the neck will 'fill out' the rein. The tension should not be so great as to become restrictive, and on no account should you pull back with either rein.

The inside rein is often overused

The job of the inside rein is to invite the horse's forehand off the track and maintain the inside bend. Many riders overuse this rein when first practising shoulder-in, sometimes opening the rein to the inside, thus creating far too much bend in the neck and virtually pulling the horse onto the forehand, making it impossible for him to walk a correct shoulder-in.

The best thing to do is to use a sponging effect of opening and closing of the fingers to create or maintain the inside flexion, if necessary. Keep both hands together as a pair with elbows rested on your torso, with the whole of your upper body in the shoulder-in position. In this way, combined with the encouragement of the inside leg, the horse will quickly understand what is required.

If this doesn't work, and he still seems confused, then the assistance of a trusted friend on the ground is invaluable.

The seat during shoulder-in

It goes without saying that a good classical seat – upright body position with expanded chest, shoulders relaxed back and down, relaxed buttocks and thigh muscles but toned and supportive abdominal and lower back muscles – is essential for correct riding of any exercise, especially shoulder-in.

The advancement of the inside hip is crucial as this will allow the horse's inside hip to advance as it needs to in this movement. It is also very important that the outside leg is taken back from the hip, not just the lower leg.

The angle of the rider's upper body, turned inwards towards the school with eyes looking that way, is also of utmost importance. This all mirrors what the horse will be doing. If you look up the track, your shoulders will inevitably turn that way, and that is when it is almost certain that the horse will not be able to keep his shoulders in off the track. The rider needs to be in shoulder-in position. When you are adept at this, it is amazing how the horse will follow you; it is a wonderful feeling!

To help in your understanding and 'feel' of this exercise, it is really helpful to walk the shoulder-in on foot. Put your hands on your hips, commence at the corner of the school, walk a small circle, and then turn up the long side. Imagine your legs are the horse's hind legs and your hips are the horse's hips. If you're 'on the left-rein', angle your upper body, that is, your shoulders, turning from the waist to the left, towards the centre of the school, and look in that direction. Progress up the track, taking your left leg in front of the right. You will feel the definite advancement of your inside (left) hip. If you then turn and look up the track, you are bound to feel most unbalanced, and it will be very difficult to continue in this position. Sylvia Loch gives some brilliant illustrations of this, as well as other exercises, in her 'Classical Seat' and 'Balance and Body Work' videos (Ref: 9.2).

Common difficulties

As in leg-yield, sometimes the rider collapses the inside hip when trying too hard to push the horse sideways. This should be avoided by thinking 'up from the waist'. Collapsing of the inside hip will result in weight being thrown onto the outside seat-bone.

It is common for a young or untrained horse to find it difficult to understand the concept of keeping his forehand off the track whilst his quarters are on the track. He then performs merely a head- and neck-in. This should be rectified by patiently and carefully following the aids as above and showing him how it's done from the ground.

Another common difficulty is that of offering a greater angle from the track as alluded to under the heading 'The misleading four-track shoulder-in'. Obviously, the horse must be discouraged from taking his forehand so far in by discreet use of the outside rein and firm body posture from the rider. The rider should keep his torso and shoulders firmly at the angle he wishes his horse's shoulders to be. It may be necessary to return to the much shallower angle of shoulder-fore, then gradually build up to shoulder-in. This should be done over weeks or months as and when the horse's strength and suppleness enable him to give the necessary bend and his back and hind legs have gained the strength to take more weight onto the haunches.

The weight aid

Previously, I have described how a discreet weight aid (the lengthening of the leg, thus weighting that particular seat-bone) in the direction of travel will encourage the horse to move that way. It is a natural aid which the horse will follow automatically in order to stay in balance with his rider.

When it comes to shoulder-in, things become a bit more complicated. Some untrained horses will benefit from the rider giving a slight weight aid with the inside leg/seat-bone initially to encourage them to bring the forehand away from the track. But the weight will then need to be centralised when the horse has responded. Sometimes a slight weight aid to the outside will reinforce the pushing aid of the inside leg to encourage the horse up the track. Obviously, the rider needs to be able to feel the reaction of the horse and respond instantaneously, otherwise the horse will be confused. If you are new to these weight aids or do not feel confident enough, then I would suggest that you keep your weight as central as possible when teaching this movement.

Making haste slowly

To 'make haste slowly' was a saying of the late Col. Alois Podhajsky and is a sentiment continued to this day by a similar motto of Arthur Kottas (a modern-day master and former Chief Rider of the Spanish Riding School), who says 'take time but don't waste time'. I cannot reiterate the importance of this philosophy too often.

As with all new exercises, just a couple of good steps in walk should be all that we are aiming for in the beginning. The horse should be amply praised for trying when he does so, even if his attempt falls short of what is required. Tact, patience and understanding are the hallmarks of good horsemanship. We must remember that all horses are slightly different, and what may come easily to some, may be difficult and take much longer for others. That's not to say that the latter won't get there in the end and be just as brilliant as those who were quick on the uptake. Some horses find some exercises particularly difficult because of conformational differences. These horses should be encouraged as it is likely that once enabled to perform the classical movements, their conformational difficulties will be greatly reduced. It is almost as much of a mistake to say 'he doesn't like that, so we won't try it again' as it is to push the horse beyond his comfort zone. There is a happy medium, and a good horseman will sense when to push or encourage (never to force) the horse to do more. Many horses thrive on new challenges. The key to my mind is to make it fun and pleasant for them so when they make the slightest improvement, they know how pleased you are. I don't rule out tit-bit treats – remember the Spanish Riding School riders have special 'sugar pockets' for such occasions when the horse has made a special effort.

Once the horse can easily perform shoulder-in at the walk, with approaching uniformity on both reins, then a few steps of trot can be introduced. The work can gradually be built-up from there over the weeks and months ahead.

One-sidedness

Remember that it is almost inevitable that any exercise will be easier on one rein than the other. This may be more noticeable when reaching the stage of shoulder-in. One reason for this is that most horses have a 'softer' and a 'harder' side, meaning that the muscles are more developed on one side of his body, or one side can stretch easier than the other. Therefore, he will find it easier to bend, say, to the right if the muscles of his left side stretch easier.

Another very common reason is that most horses have one hind leg which is stronger than the other. Therefore, if this stronger hind leg is his right hind, then he will find shoulder-in on the right rein much easier because it is the right hind which does most of the driving of the weight to the left. This is vice versa in some of the other lateral movements, but we will discuss this later when we reach that stage.

This one-sidedness is quite normal, so one should not be too concerned about it, but it does need to be addressed. To make the horse 'straight' in a dressage sense is to enable him to perform all exercises with equal bend on both reins. There are virtually no horses who are completely or exactly 'equal' or 'straight', but when fully trained, the difference should be hardly noticeable. Shoulder-in is one of the exercises which will help immensely to this end, but don't get downhearted if the difference from one rein to the other continues for some time.

Progressing the exercise programme

Don't forget to intersperse your lateral steps with plenty of forward movement in trot or canter, and never forget to give the horse (and yourself) plenty of breaks on a long rein to rest and perhaps think about what you have just achieved. When first teaching shoulder-in, just a few attempts on each rein are enough in one session. Try to finish on a positive note. Never over-face the green horse; try to make training pleasurable for him and yourself.

Shoulder-in, as most exercises, should be practised in walk for some time before progressing to the trot. Just a few strides of trot is sufficient in the early stages; this can be very gradually built up until the horse can perform shoulder-in right down the long side of the arena. It won't be for some time later in the training when you can carry on the shoulder-in around the corner of the school as this is a lot more strenuous. You should be able to feel when the horse finds it easier and is more than willing to progress further.

Shoulder-in at the canter?

Although shoulder-in at the walk is very good for building strength and flexibility, both in the horse's back, quarters and hind leg joints, its main use is usually in the trot. It can be ridden in canter, but this is extremely strenuous and demanding, and I would not recommend any attempt at this until a very advanced stage of training, if at all. Some classical masters do not use canter shoulder-in at all, whilst others do. Here is what Col. Podhajsky says, so canter shoulder-in was clearly not used when he was Director of the SRS (Ref: 9.3):

The renvers and half-pass can be executed in all three paces, whereas the shoulder-in can be executed only in the walk or trot and the full travers only from the halt.

I think that what some people refer to as shoulder-in at the canter is actually shoulder-fore, which is a lot more understandable.

Shoulder-in brings about unity

Once you and your horse can execute shoulder-in smoothly and easily, utilising the weight and body aids as described in this chapter, you will find every other part of your riding will be better, lighter and more harmonious. Whilst out hacking, your horse should be more responsive, lighter in the forehand, easier to turn and a lot less likely to trip or fall. You will be well on the way to complete unity between you and your equine partner.

Remember that it may be some time, possibly years, before the movement can be executed equally well on both reins (because of natural one-sidedness), but given time and patience, gradually the difference will become barely noticeable.

References

Ref: 9.1 – 'School of Horsemanship' – de la Guérinière, Francois Robichon – Translated by Tracy Boucher – J.A. Allen – 2003.

Ref: 9.2 – 'The Classical Seat' & 'Balance & Bodywork' – DVD's – Loch, Sylvia – Available from Sylvia Loch, Long Meadow, Tilbury Juxta Clare, Sudbury, CO9 4JT.

Ref: 9.3 – 'The Complete Training of Horse and Rider' – Podhajsky, Col. Alois – Translated by Eva Podhajsky & Col. V.D.S. Williams – Harrap – 1967.

The travers or quarters-in

10

After the demi-pirouette and shoulder-in, the travers (pronounced 'tra-vare') is the next logical step on the ladder of classical exercises. Although there is no definitive order in which the exercises should be taught, it is definitely best to teach shoulder-in before the other lateral movements.

Travers and renvers (renvers is where the forehand is brought in from the track as in shoulder-in but with the opposite bend; pronounced 'ron-vare') are very similar exercises and can be thought of as mirror images of each other. Some people incorrectly say that travers and half-pass are virtually the same exercise. I say that this is incorrect as, when we consider the movements of the half-pass, they are quite different. In half-pass, the horse is moving forward and sideways at the same time; both front and hind legs criss-cross. In travers and renvers, the front legs will never criss-cross, and the shoulders stay parallel to a straight line. The horse is not moving forward in the same way as the half-pass but sideways on a different bias. Although there may be similarities, they are quite different exercises.

Some trainers do not use travers at all, especially with some horses who are particularly crooked. Basically, in travers, the forehand stays on the track, whilst the quarters are brought in from the track by about 30 degrees, bent around the rider's inside leg, travelling sideways in the direction of the bend. Obviously, when first teaching the travers, a smaller degree of displacement from the track will be asked.

Since a lot of horses have a tendency to swing their quarters inwards to avoid the extra work of bending correctly, and because they are naturally crooked (one-sided), it is easy to see the logic of not teaching the travers at all. Why teach the horse to do something which you are normally trying to dissuade him from doing?

DOI: 10.1201/9781003503422-11

There is also a logical argument for leaving the travers until later in training when the horse is straighter and less inclined to swing the quarters when not required. It's all a matter of what you find best for your particular horse. There is no hard and fast rule.

Travers can be a good preparation for half-pass

Having said all the above, I do find travers a good preparation for half-pass as long as it is not making the horse more crooked. Half-pass is more difficult and requires more collection than travers, so I find it can help give him an inkling of what is required without quite so much effort.

As with shoulder-in, travers can be practised anywhere in the school, but it is much easier and preferable to begin training it on the track of the arena. Here we will have the wall of the school to help us contain the movement and keep the sideways travel, impeding any forward progression. This makes it easier not only for the rider to aid but also for the horse to understand what is being asked.

The horse's body movements in travers

In shoulder-in, we ask for the shoulder to come off the track and for the horse to bend around the rider's inside leg, with the hind legs travelling down the track (see Chapter 9). For the travers, we ask that the horse keep his forehand travelling down the track, still bent around the rider's inside leg, but this time, we ask him to bring his quarters in from the track, travelling sideways in the direction of the bend (whereas in shoulder-in he is travelling away from the direction of bend).

Some horses take to this exercise like the proverbial 'duck to water', whereas other horse and rider combinations struggle with it unduly. The key here is to maintain the bend, which needs to be from poll to tail, not just an inside flexion of the head and neck. It is so difficult for the horse to perform the movement with a straight body, and for this reason, I feel it imperative that the horse has fully mastered the shoulder-in beforehand, with the accompanying ability to bend from poll to tail.

The aim eventually is to bring the quarters in from the track at about a 30-degree angle – the same as for a normal three-track shoulder-in. However, in the same way as we begin shoulder-in with the lesser angle of shoulder-fore (that is with the shoulder only just off the track), we also begin the travers with the quarters just a little in from the track, thus, making it easier

Figure 10.1 The Travers

This shows the footfalls of the travers, with the appropriate displacement from the track of 30 degrees and appropriate bend from poll to tail into the direction of bend along the track. The wall of the school is the straight line on the left. Figure courtesy of Lesley Skipper.

for the horse in the beginning. The greater angle from the track requires greater flexibility and bend from poll to tail, as well as more collection. Also, in the same way as shoulder-in, travers assists with the development of collection; the quality of the travers improves as the collection improves. Therefore, one complements the other.

Head to the wall or full-pass

Some trainers like to use a greater degree angle of quarters-in, often as a warm-up exercise. This is usually termed 'head to the wall' or 'full-pass'. At this greater angle, it is virtually impossible for the horse to bend throughout his body, and all that is required is an inside flexion. I am not a great fan of this movement as it has none of the benefits of true travers, or quarters-in, and I feel it can serve to discourage the requirement to bend his body. This greater angle from the track is often offered by the horse in the beginning of training in order to avoid the bend and as a way of straightening his body to make it easy for himself. I therefore feel that it should not be encouraged. This is very similar to the scenario of too great an angle of shoulder-in which is often offered by the novice horse in order to avoid bending his body.

The differences in the driving leg which equates to the direction of travel

It is important to understand that in the right rein shoulder-in, where the horse is travelling *away* from the bend, the *driving leg is the right hind*. In the right rein travers, the horse moves *into* the direction of the bend, and his *driving leg is the left hind*.

This explains why many horses will find right rein shoulder-in easy, but they may struggle with right rein travers. Whereas on the left rein, they may find the opposite – left shoulder-in may be more difficult than left travers. This is usually because their right hind is stronger than their left. With other horses, of course, the opposite may well be the case. Most horses begin training with one hind leg stronger than the other. This, combined with a tendency to bend easier in their bodies in one direction than the other – that is, the muscles on one side of the body are more developed than the other – makes for what is termed a 'one-sided' or 'crooked' horse. One of the main aims of the classical exercises is to supple and strengthen the muscles, joints and tendons equally on both sides to create what we term a 'straight' horse. In this way, lateral exercises aim to straighten the horse, as well as help him collect, lighten his forehand and take more weight onto the strong hindquarters. This relieves the precious front legs, making the horse much lighter in hand and more pleasurable to ride, and it should substantially increase his chances of a sound, healthy and long life.

Don't do too much too soon

All these beneficial effects are of course wonderful and a joy both to ride and behold. BUT beware – some riders and trainers are in too much of a hurry, and doing too much too soon, especially when the horse is unfit or too young, can have the opposite effect. If the horse is in any way forced or coerced into performing these movements, they cease to be beneficial exercises and can cause strain, particularly to the hocks, fetlocks and tendons.

Always begin new exercises in walk

Start the travers as you did with shoulder-in, and every new exercise: in walk. Just ask for a stride or two at first, then ride straight again; gradually building up the number of steps and degree of angle until the horse finds it easier.

The rider's aids for travers

It is best to begin to ask for travers on the track just after the second corner of the short side of the arena, just before commencing travel down the long side.

Here we will assume you are on the right rein: give a short, gentle, half-halt just before the corner to balance the horse; your left leg should be behind the girth at the corner. Deepen your right (inside) leg as you come around the corner, and make sure that the whole of your left (outside) leg, from the hip downwards, is definitely back. Keep the right bend created on the corner, if necessary, by gently squeezing or engaging in a give and take of the fingers of the right (inside) hand, but ensure that you support the horse's left shoulder with the left (outside) rein – this is important. On no account should you pull with either rein, and keep your hands together at the withers.

Your right hip should be in advance of your left, and your upper body, including your head, shoulders and torso, should be positioned where you want your horse's head and shoulders. In other words, your shoulders and hips should be a mirror image of your horse's, or vice versa. You need to be looking where you want your horse to look, with your shoulders angled towards the wall of the school/down the track.

Your outside leg gives the aid to request the quarters to move inwards, and your body posture and hands guide the forehand into the correct position.

It is quite likely that the first step or two will be faltering and difficult. This is only to be expected. Praise the horse at every attempt he makes to comply with your request, then ride straight forward again.

Starting from shoulder-in

It is sometimes easier for the horse to understand what is required if you begin with a couple of strides of shoulder-in, which he should, by this stage, be well acquainted with.

The leg and seat aids for travers are very similar in many ways as those for shoulder-in. Your right (inside) hip is already forward, and your left (outside) leg and hip are back. In the shoulder-in, your shoulders and torso are turned in, and you are looking in towards the centre of the school. To ask for travers, turn your upper body from the waist, taking your hands as a pair back towards the wall of the school. Turn your head at the same time, and look towards the wall / down the track.

Keep your upper body tall and erect with an expanded chest, elbows gently resting on your sides, making sure you keep the right bend. Make sure you don't overdo the left (outside) rein, which could well turn the horse's head to the left, or interfere with the right bend. Just keep the right amount of support in the outside rein; keeping your hands together as a pair should help with this.

Your left (outside) leg makes the request for the quarters to move to the right at the exact moment that you make the turn with your upper body. Your right (inside) leg becomes passive but remains supportive; it is now the pillar which the horse is bending around and moving towards. Your left leg discreetly requests the sideways movement and maintains the quarters-in position with either a gentle pushing movement or an on / off vibratory aid.

Continuing the training

In the beginning of training, don't push the horse into performing travers all the way up the track, even if he appears to find it easy. As with all new exercises, just practise it on both reins say two or three times in each training session.

At first it is likely to be much easier on one rein than the other, but with tact and patience this difference should gradually become less noticeable. After a number of weeks of regularly practising this new exercise, and when it has become easy in walk, you can then commence a few strides in trot.

Obviously, for reasons already discussed, travers should not be practised too often with horses who already have a tendency to throw their quarters in, usually on one particular rein. However, this crookedness can usually be corrected by the appropriate use of other lateral movements.

Moving from shoulder-in to travers then back to shoulder-in is a very good exercise to create impulsion, and this can be carried out both in walk and trot once the horse is strong and supple enough to find it easy. Always build up the number of strides gradually week by week, depending on your horse's fitness and aptitude. Don't neglect the other work; it is still important that you can ride straight and practise bends and circles.

As mentioned previously, there are varying views as to which exercises should be carried out at the canter. I am inclined to the view that shoulder-in and travers should only be ridden in walk and trot, and not in canter, but I do not strongly disagree with canter being used in these exercises, when the horse is suitably advanced and prepared.

Half-pass

11

After the shoulder-in and travers, or quarters-in, which we looked at in previous chapters, half-pass is the next logical step on the lateral ladder.

Many people teach renvers before half-pass. This is fine if it works for your horse, but I find it to be particularly difficult with many horses, so it is also fine to leave it until the other exercises are confirmed.

It is also perfectly possible to teach half-pass after shoulder-in, omitting travers altogether. However, as mentioned before, I find travers a good preparation for half-pass as long as the horse is not being encouraged to swing his quarters in when not required.

We have already discussed the differences and similarities of travers and half-pass, so now we are going to ask the horse to move forward and sideways at the same time, bent in the direction of the movement (unlike shoulder-in, where he is moving away from the direction of the movement). This may be quite a difficult concept for the horse to understand at first, and it certainly requires more strength than travers or renvers. It is essential that shoulder-in is firmly established first.

Half-pass requires, as well as creates, more collection, on the part of the horse. It therefore follows that the horse must be appropriately fit and prepared before commencement of this exercise.

The horse's movements in half-pass

The horse should move simultaneously forwards and laterally, bent towards the direction of travel and bent around the rider's inside leg.

DOI: 10.1201/9781003503422-12

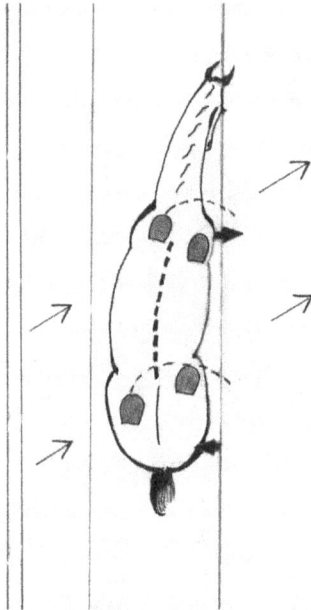

Figure 11.1 The Half-Pass

This figure shows the footfalls of the half-pass together with the degree of bend and positioning of the horse's body in relation to the wall of the school (the straight line on the left). The horse is moving forward and sideways, into the direction of the bend. Figure courtesy of Lesley Skipper.

The forehand should precede the quarters by about half a stride. This point, together with the forward momentum, is important. If both or either of these principles are lost, then the exercise will become more akin to a full-pass, which does not create the same amount of suppleness and strengthening benefits as half-pass. The full-pass also does not require nor create collection and weight carrying of the haunches as does half-pass. The full-pass is where the horse moves only sideways into the bend. It is sometimes taught as a manoeuvre to police horses for crowd control purposes.

Both the horse's front and hind legs will cross over in half-pass. For instance, in left half-pass the right fore will step in front of and cross over the left fore. The right hind will step in front of and across the left hind towards the horse's centre of gravity, pushing the horse forwards and sideways. Thus, the outside hind (as in travers) is the driving leg, and the one which does most of the work and is therefore strengthened and suppled.

As I keep reiterating, we must remember that most horses have a stiff and a more supple side, as well as one hind leg which is stronger than the other. The two are not necessarily on the same side. It is quite possible to have a horse who bends easier to the right but whose left hind is the weaker side. Such a horse will find right half-pass the more difficult one because, although he can bend easily to the right, his left hind finds it harder to drive the movement. This horse will find right shoulder-in easier than left because in shoulder-in it will be the right (inside) hind driving the movement.

It is important to practise any exercise on both reins – not just the one which the horse finds easy – but it makes sense to teach the half-pass in the beginning on the side which the horse finds easiest. Then, once it is fully understood by the horse, a stride or two on the difficult rein can be practised, obviously only in walk to begin with.

However, it must be borne in mind that these exercises are, even when carried out in walk, quite strenuous and should not be practised to excess, especially in the early days of training. The horse must be afforded patience and empathy if he finds it difficult in the early days. He must *never be forced*. The least little bit of understanding and co-operation on the part of the horse should be liberally praised.

It should be much easier for the horse, both to understand and to physically carry out the half-pass, once he is well used to the shoulder-in and travers and can perform these two exercises with ease.

Differences and similarities to leg-yield

Some people find it easier to understand the movement of the half-pass by thinking of it as a reverse leg-yield. It does have definite similarities in that the horse moves forwards and sideways at the same time, with the forehand in advance of the quarters by about half a stride.

The big difference is that the bend is reversed. In leg-yield, the horse is moving away from the bend, or flexion, which is all that is required, whereas in half-pass, he is bent in the direction in which he is travelling. Leg-yield is a much easier exercise and the first lateral movement we teach, therefore, a uniform bend from poll to tail is not required.

In half-pass, the bend should be equal from poll to tail. The bend does not have to be too great, but it does need to be a uniformed bend. It is virtually impossible, and would be incorrect, to perform it without any bend at all.

The similarities between the two exercises end there. Leg-yield is merely a movement which helps to supple and balance the horse, at the same time teaching him to move away from the rider's unilateral leg aid. It does not require, nor create, collection and the extra weight-bearing capacity of the haunches as does half-pass. As mentioned before, leg-yield is not essential, but I find it quite useful. Some people may think that it confuses the horse, but this has never been my experience. With a sensitive rider, giving clear aids, the horse soon learns to move forwards and sideways with a different bend. I believe that leg-yield is a good preparatory movement for the lateral exercises and a good warm-up exercise in walk for advanced horses.

With more advanced horses whose half-pass is well established, riding half-pass, changing to leg-yield and back again is a good exercise to keep the horse supple, quick off the aids and interested in the lesson.

The amount of bend the horse is capable of in half-pass will differ with each horse, depending on conformation and stage of training. I would suggest that when first teaching the half-pass, it is best to ask for a little bend, so long as it is from poll to tail and not merely head and neck. Here's what Arthur Kottas (former Chief Rider at the SRS) says about half-pass in his book *Kottas on Dressage* (Ref: 11.1):

> Each horse has a degree of bend that suits him. The stronger the horse, the greater the bend will be. With young horses the degree of bend will be less. . . . The bend of a horse is not the same on both reins when he has one strongly concave and one strongly convex side. Minimizing such one-sidedness is part of the suppling process of training, in which astute use of the lateral exercises plays a part. As the horse becomes more supple laterally, half-pass (and much else) becomes easier. In general, when stiffness arises, one has exceeded the degree to which the horse can currently bend correctly on that side.

The rider's aids for half-pass (right rein in this case)

It is a good idea to ride either a shoulder-in or travers down the long side of the school to improve the collection before commencing the first strides of half-pass. Presuming that you are on the right rein, you could ride a shoulder-in then change to travers at the halfway marker down the long side. Straighten the horse at the corner (i.e., change to a normal bend) and give a gentle half-halt. At about the quarter line (halfway before reaching the centre line) on the short side of the school, turn off the track to the right. You are aiming to ride forward and sideways back to the track from whence you came, with the horse bent around your right leg. If you begin at the quarter line, you will not have too far to ride before reaching the track, which is less daunting than starting at the halfway line.

Leg, torso and weight aids

For half-pass, right step slightly into your right stirrup, and bend the horse around your right (inside) leg, which should give support and encourage the bend. Turn your shoulders in the direction you wish your horse to position his shoulders; bring your right shoulder very slightly back. Your left (outside) leg should be taken back from the hip, not just from the knee.

As the horse moves off the track, ask with your left (outside) leg for the sideways movement to the right. It is important to do this at the point of leaving the track before the horse has straightened up. In order to differentiate the outside leg aid from that of canter, try making the pushing aid slowly and gently. At the same time as the left leg requests the movement of the quarters, the left (outside) rein must back up this aid (see following 'Rein aids' section).

Be careful not to try too hard to push the horse over with your outside leg, nor to step too far into the inside stirrup. Both these mistakes can cause a rider to collapse at the hip, causing weight to be transferred to the outside seat-bone, seriously confusing the horse and hampering his lateral steps.

Look where you want your horse to look, that is slightly in the direction of the half-pass. Your shoulders will also be very slightly angled that way, so your shoulders will be parallel to that of the horse. It almost goes without saying that you need to be in a good classical seat. Sit tall with your chest expanded, tummy and lower back muscles toned, but without stiffness; shoulders should be relaxed back and down with elbows resting against your side and thumbs on top of the reins with a straight line from your elbow to the horse's mouth. This straight line can be downwards, not necessarily horizontal.

Rein aids

Your right (inside) rein indicates the direction of bend but must definitely not be overused or opened to the right. This would pull the horse onto the right shoulder and overbend the neck.

It is imperative that the left (outside) rein is held against the horse's neck to both support and indicate the degree of lateral steps.

Keep both hands together just above the withers; take them to the right slightly so that the left rein is against the horse's neck, but don't allow your left hand to move over to the right of the withers.

A tactful sponging of the fingers of the right rein may be required to indicate to the horse that he should be bending to the right.

The left (outside) rein is key to the degree of lateral steps. If you use too much left rein, then the movement will cease to go forwards and will merely move sideways, thus losing much of the physical benefits of the exercise. The forward movement must take precedence over the sideways steps. However, if too little support is given by the left (outside) rein, then the horse will most likely walk in a straight diagonal line back to the track, losing the half-pass altogether.

There should *never be any pulling with the reins*. All rein aids should be given with tact and sympathy, and your hands should work in conjunction with all the other aids so they are never in isolation.

You will soon know if you are using too much outside rein because you will feel the horse losing forward momentum, so just ease with this rein, without giving it away altogether, encouraging the forward movement with your right leg gently at the girth. If you give the outside rein too much, the horse will feel abandoned and confused.

Keeping the forehand preceding the quarters (by about half a stride)

This can be very tricky when first teaching half-pass. You may feel that the quarters swing inwards to the right and then get 'left behind' to the left. This is to be expected at first, and you must try to feel where the quarters are and adjust the amount of left (outside) leg pressure needed, which will vary from moment to moment, until the horse understands the movement. Try not to overuse your outside leg; use the minimum aid possible. It is always easier to increase the aid than to correct an over-strong aid. When he is established in half-pass, of course, your aids should be almost imperceptible.

At first you may feel like it is a bit of a juggling act, but practice and patience makes perfect.

Tilting of the horse's head

A common problem during half-pass is one of tilting of the horse's head. This may be because the rein tension is not equal; the inside rein may be too tight. Try supporting a little more with the outside rein, softening slightly the inside rein and gently using the inside leg intermittently.

Don't do too much too soon

As with all new exercises, always begin training in walk. Just a stride or two will suffice in the beginning, and then ride straight forward again. Practise on both reins, and bear in mind that one rein will be easier than the other.

Give the horse some leeway for these imperfections until he has had time to build up his strength, suppleness and general ability. With time and patience, these inconsistencies will become less noticeable.

It may be many weeks or even months before the horse is ready to advance to performing half-pass in trot, and possibly years before he is capable of doing it in canter. Let the horse dictate your timetable; take as long as it takes. It will be worth it in the end. If you try to do too much too soon, you will have left the ethos of the classical school, and you will most likely be damaging your horse for life and losing the beauty and harmony that could have been yours. Both you and your horse should enjoy the journey as much as the destination.

Reference

Ref: 11.1 – 'Kottas on Dressage' – Kottas-Heldenberg, Arthur & Rowbotham, Julie – Kenilworth Press – 2010.

Renvers or haunches out

12

Renvers is more difficult than Travers or even than Shoulder-in. For this reason the rider should demand only a few steps to commence with and mainly concentrate on the regular fluent movement of the horse.

– from *The Complete Training of Horse and Rider* by Col. Alois Podhajsky (Ref: 12.1)

I begin this chapter with the quote from Col. Podhajsky's book to impress upon people that they should neither expect nor demand too much too soon, particularly with this difficult exercise.

The renvers (pronounced 'ron-vare') is the last in the classical lateral exercises. It is sometimes referred to as haunches-out or tail to the wall. It is really the twin exercise to travers, although a little different. The main difference lies in the position in which the exercises are executed, in particular, their relationship to the wall or a straight line.

The horse's movement in renvers

To understand the biomechanics of renvers, it is helpful to first think of the horse's position in shoulder-in, say on the right rein.

In shoulder-in right, the horse's quarters are on the track with the forehand brought in from the track and the horse bent right from poll to tail around the rider's right leg, moving away from the direction of the bend. To produce renvers from shoulder-in, the positioning of the quarters on the track and forehand in from the track remain the same. The difference is that the bend is changed, so the horse is bent to the left from poll to tail,

DOI: 10.1201/9781003503422-13

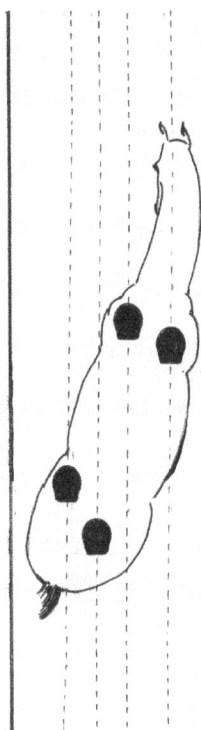

Figure 12.1 The Renvers

This figure shows the footfall of the renvers, together with the degree of bend and position of the horse's body in relation to the wall of the school (the straight line on the left). The horse is moving into the direction of the bend. Figure courtesy of Lesley Skipper.

bending around the rider's left leg, moving towards the direction of the bend.

The horse's driving hind leg also remains the same. In right shoulder-in, it is the right hind which steps in front of the left (towards the centre of gravity of the horse). In renvers, the hind leg action remains the same (although the horse is bent to the left, that is, bent towards the direction of travel, whereas in shoulder-in he is bent away from the direction of travel); it is still the right hind which steps forward and under, driving the movement. In this way, it is similar to half-pass. In travers or quarters-in, although the bend remains the same as in shoulder-in, the driving hind leg changes; so, in right travers, the horse's left hind leg becomes the driving leg, as it is in right half-pass.

If all this sounds very complicated, if you study the overhead diagrams and think about the footfalls, it should become clear.

Here is what Paul Belasik has to say on the matter in his book *Dressage for the 21st Century* (Ref: 12.2):

> There is no better preparation for the half-pass than travers and renvers, and there are no better exercises for correcting faults in the half-pass. In regard to this, some trainers have said that the half-pass is nothing more than a renvers or travers on a diagonal line. This points to a misunderstanding of the lateral exercises. The travers and renvers have a specific relationship to a line or a wall. That is, the shoulders are parallel to that line or wall. It does not matter in which direction that line travels – diagonal (across the arena), or along the wall – it is still a straight line and the shoulders stay parallel to it. Obviously, in travers and renvers the forefeet will never criss-cross or scissor as they will in half-pass, so the latter is a very different exercise.

My personal view is that renvers, because of its difficulty, should not be introduced until after half-pass has been well established, but I do find that travers can be a useful precursor to half-pass.

The rider's aids for renvers

A useful way of introducing renvers is to create it from shoulder-in since you already have the required positioning of the quarters on the track and the forehand in from the track at the required angle of approximately 30 degrees (although I would advise that you allow a shallower angle from the track when introducing the exercise).

Renvers on the right rein

I would suggest that you ride, say, on the right rein, a walk shoulder-in for about three-quarters of the way down the long side of the school. The horse should be very well established in shoulder-in before attempting renvers, so this length of shoulder-in should be no problem.

Remember that when creating renvers from shoulder-in (or simply on the right rein), you are changing the bend; therefore, if you ride it from the right rein, the left side becomes the inside until you change back to a right bend.

In dressage terms, the inside is always the inside of the bend.

When you are about three-quarters of the way down the long side, change your leg aids. In shoulder-in right, the horse is bent around your right leg on the girth with your left leg behind the girth. You now need to change the bend to the left (the left side becoming the new inside), so gently ask for a change of bend with your left hand in a sponging motion, which asks the horse to look left. At the same time, reverse your leg aids. Bring your left leg forward and slide your right leg back. Your left leg has now become the inside leg which you request that the horse should bend around, and your right leg slightly behind the girth controls the quarters and tactfully drives the movement to the left, in a similar way as in left half-pass.

The rider should gently apply the outside rein (in right rein renvers, this will be the right rein) in order to support the horse and control the amount of bend in his neck. The left rein (which in right rein renvers will be the inside rein) affirms the flexion to the left as and when necessary. Be careful not to overbend the neck; remember that the bend should be uniform from poll to tail.

As mentioned previously, when first teaching the exercise, it is best to ask for a smaller displacement of the shoulders from the track. So, if you were riding a shoulder-in at roughly a 30-degree angle, just allow the forehand to come further towards the track in order to make it easier for the horse in the beginning.

You must simultaneously change your body posture and weight aid. Your left hip needs to be advanced, and your head and shoulder position should change very slightly to mirror the position you require from the horse.

You should make a slight weight aid to your inside seat-bone (in this case your left). Some people find that this is easily done by thinking of slightly weighting the inside stirrup, which automatically puts a little extra weight on the inside seat-bone. Although your inside leg will need to come slightly forward to stay underneath your advanced inside hip, try not to brace your left foot against the stirrup, forcing it too far forward. If this happens, your left leg will cease to support the horse on the bend.

As in all these exercises, you must keep your upper body supported, tall and upright to avoid any collapsing at the hip.

If you manage a few steps of renvers before reaching the corner of the school, be very pleased and praise your horse. Change back to a right bend well before reaching the corner. If the horse is struggling and you only manage one or two steps, don't worry. Simply return to a right bend, bringing your left leg and hip slightly back again and right leg forward to the 'on the girth position', and ride straight on the track, making the right turn at the corner as normal.

Other ways of approaching renvers

Shoulder-in, travers and renvers can all be ridden on the circle, and although difficult to ride accurately, some horses may find this a helpful introduction to this new exercise.

Renvers can also be ridden on an oblique line across the school, but in this case, it is very difficult for the rider to keep the horse correctly positioned. When ridden on the track, the quarters are supported by the wall, and the movement is usually much more accurate.

Another way of introducing renvers is to begin after a half-pass. To do this, ride a half-pass, say, from the three-quarter line on the right rein towards the track to your right. You should reach the track before the halfway marker of 'E' or 'B'. Before reaching the track, ask for the renvers instead of straightening the horse and continuing along the track. In other words, you keep the forehand to the left (before the quarters reach the track), then take the quarters to the track and keep the right bend in the renvers position.

The uses of renvers and when to introduce it

As already established, renvers is generally considered to be the most difficult of the lateral exercises and should not be attempted until the horse is very supple and strong in his haunches and hind leg joints. If you find it to be too demanding at first, just leave it for some time (possibly a few months), and make another attempt after further gradual strengthening and suppling have been carried out.

Never ask for any new exercise in trot until it is well established in walk. When the horse can perform renvers easily for say half the length of the long side of the school in walk, then you can ask for a few strides of trot, but don't be surprised if this is more difficult. If needed, return to practising in walk until the exercise is more established.

Renvers is very good for suppling and strengthening the haunches. It can be ridden in walk or trot and is a very demanding exercise when carried out in canter. Renvers in canter should not be attempted until the horse is established in canter half-pass.

Renvers confirms the lateral bend and adds another dimension to the array of exercises available to the rider/trainer. Intertwining exercises, without concentrating on one particular movement for too long, adds interest and keeps both horse and rider mentally and physically engrossed and in tune with each other. If the horse is enjoying his training, as he should be, he will be keenly listening to the next change of body posture or aiding request from the rider. The rider, for his part, must be mindful of any difficulties that the horse is encountering and not ask too much too soon, nor be too insistent on immediate obedience if there is a possibility that the horse either does not understand or is experiencing a physical difficulty. We must always listen to our horses so that they can listen to us.

Also, remember my personal motto: we aim to strengthen and supple the horse, not to stress him, either mentally or physically.

References

Ref: 12.1 – 'The Complete Training of Horse and Rider' – Podhajsky, Col. Alois – Translated by Eva Podhajsky & Col. V.D.S. Williams – Harrap – 1967.

Ref: 12.2 – 'Dressage for the 21st Century' – Belasik, Paul – J.A. Allen – 2001.

Rein-back

13

Including position of the rider's lower leg for different movements

The rein-back, when used as a training exercise, is an advanced and extremely strenuous exercise. I would not recommend its introduction until the horse is fairly strong in the back and hindquarters and the joints of his hind limbs are strengthened and flexible. He needs to be capable of a fair degree of collection, meaning he can take weight back onto the haunches. Of course, when it is practised well, this exercise will greatly enhance the strength in this regard, but it should not be attempted too soon as a bad rein-back will do no good at all.

It's a different matter to ask the horse to move back for practical purposes when in hand, or perhaps manoeuvring round a gate, in which case all that is asked is a few shuffling steps backward. This can, and should, be asked from a very early stage. You can make very good use of the word 'back' whilst in the stable, accompanied by a gentle tap or push on the chest. When the horse is used to this verbal command, it will help greatly when asking for the rein-back under saddle.

I deplore the practice of 'training' the horse to move backwards by using a long line in hand and waggling/shaking the line until he backs away from it. This is most uncomfortable and stressful for the horse and causes him to back up with a raised head and hollow back; this is not good at all and the opposite of what we are aiming for.

When you think your horse's muscles and joints are sufficiently strengthened, and he is advanced enough in his training to begin rein-back proper, the first thing to do is to make a good square halt on the track. It is

DOI: 10.1201/9781003503422-14

often useful to have a kindly friend on the ground who can encourage the horse backwards without frightening him.

In a correct rein-back under saddle, the horse makes distinct steps back with diagonal footfalls, in the same way as in trot, unlike the four-beat forward walk. The feet should be raised and moved smoothly backwards and not dragged. Of course, we are not expecting perfection to begin with.

The aids for the rein-back

Start from an active, but not fast, walk – as collected as the horse can be.

Come to a smooth and balanced halt, as described in Chapter 5. If the horse is not square, that is, with both hind and forelegs parallel to each other, then walk on and try again. You may need the help of your friend on the ground just to nudge a hind leg forward to bring it in line with the opposite hind (it is the hind legs which are often misaligned).

At this point, you need to have a definite yet fairly light contact with the horse's mouth, and the horse should be standing to attention.

Whilst sitting very tall and upright, with an expanded chest, incline your upper torso slightly forward, thus lifting your weight off the back of the saddle. Be very careful not to collapse at the waist as this would throw your weight forward onto the horse's shoulders, throwing him out of balance. Keeping an expanded chest and strong abdominal muscles should avoid any collapsing. I have found that, in the early training, it is sometimes helpful to increase the degree of forward inclination of the upper torso, and this can be minimised later on.

At the same time as inclining your upper torso forward, apply your lower legs slightly back from the usual 'on the girth' position. Sylvia Loch's essential book *The Classical Seat* (Ref: 13.1) shows a brilliant, crystal-clear diagram of what she terms 'the panel of buttons' on the horse's side. This shows how and where different lower leg positions of the rider will give a different signal to the horse. These are not buttons which the horse has to learn by rote; they are based on sound physiological facts (the intercostal nerves which stimulate different movements; see diagram in Chapter 6), whereby certain nerves under the skin will prompt a different action of the horse. This is a completely natural and kind way to aid the horse.

You can see from the photos that 'button B' is the correct placing of the leg when asking for rein-back. It is also the one used unilaterally by the outside leg for canter, lateral work and turns, so it is important that when used for rein-back, both legs are applied at the same time. It is also

Figure 13.1 Button A

This shows the correct 'on-the-girth' position for all forward movement and impulsion. Photo courtesy of Lesley Skipper.

Figure 13.2 Button B

This shows the correct position of the leg for lateral work, turns, outside leg in canter and rein-back. The rider should be careful not to use the leg too far back, which would cause the horse confusion (see button D). Photo courtesy of Lesley Skipper.

Figure 13.3 Button C

This shows the correct position of the leg to stimulate the muscles which extend the foreleg for extension. Photo courtesy of Lesley Skipper.

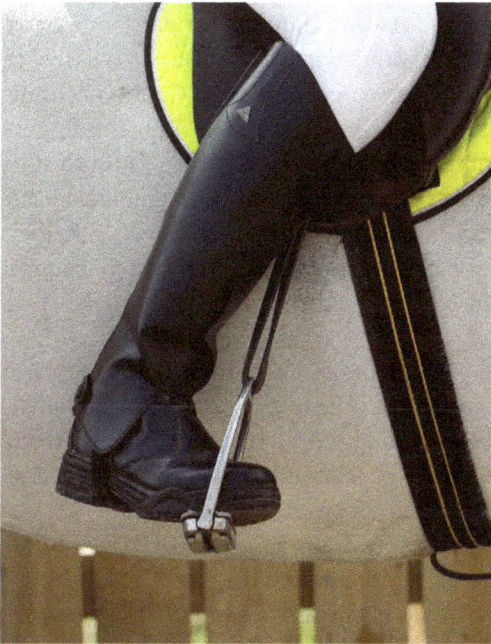

Figure 13.4 Button D

This shows the correct position of the leg for requesting elevation, such as passage and piaffe. It is further back than button B and should be used with discretion. Photo courtesy of Lesley Skipper.

important not to use the leg too far back, which would be stimulating 'button D'. This is the nerve which we stimulate when asking for elevation, such as in passage and piaffe. Be careful not to use your leg too far back. Here is what Lesley Skipper says in her book *Exercise School for Horse and Rider* (Ref: 13.2):

> Finally, there is button D, which lies behind button B and is used for elevated work such as passage and piaffe. (Bear in mind, however, that, as we have seen, stimulating the nerves too far back may tip the horse onto his forehand, so for most riders this 'button' is perhaps best left alone).

I strongly recommend that you also refer to *The Classical Seat* by Sylvia Loch (Ref: 13.1).

We must also bear in mind that horses are not machines, and they may not, in the initial stages, respond to these stimuli, for various reasons. If they are tense, the muscles and nerves will not respond, and they may take a while to become accustomed to this aiding. Nevertheless, it is a completely natural thing for them to respond to, and they will respond to these natural aids much faster than any artificial 'cue'.

If the horse does not immediately understand that he should move back, and he begins to move forward, then the forward impulsion should be 'held' by the reins. If this is all done with discretion, he will feel the impulsion aid, and there is nowhere else to go but back. On no account should you pull backwards. You can use a gentle 'ask' through the fingers, requesting the backward step, but if the contact on the horse's mouth starts to become too strong, it is better to abandon the rein-back and ask him to move forward. Of course, this can be immensely helped by your helper on the ground, who, at the point of him misunderstanding and wanting to move forward, can put a hand on his chest. Also, the voice request of 'back' should be a great help.

At first the backward steps are likely to be hesitant, possibly just dragging or shuffling backwards, but if he is moving backwards at all, be very pleased, and reward him verbally and with a stroke. Don't ask for more than one or two strides at first, and immediately move forward again, although not too abruptly as this could be perceived as a rebuke.

Don't practise this more than a couple of times in any one schooling session. As time goes on, possibly weeks or even months, you should find that your horse will step backwards correctly and smoothly using diagonal pairs of legs, with very little feel on the rein. In fact, eventually you can do it with no rein contact at all!

Releasing the aids

It is imperative that the rider's aids should be released at the moment the rein-back is required to cease. Return your upper torso to the usual upright position, and return your lower legs to the 'on the girth' position, easing any feel on the rein. You are then ready to apply your lower legs in the correct position for forward movement again.

How not to rein-back

Some really dreadful sights of rein-back can be seen, especially in films, with riders leaning back and pulling on the reins. The poor horses' heads are pulled upwards towards the sky and their backs and necks are in a banana shape. I can think of nothing worse nor more damaging. To my mind, this kind of riding amounts to real cruelty.

Things that can go wrong

Ideally, the horse should move backwards in a completely straight line, but as in all things, at first things don't always go that smoothly. When the horse is struggling a bit, he will probably shuffle back, swinging his quarters one way or another. This is where it is essential to halt alongside a fence and helpful to have someone on the ground to dissuade the quarters from swinging inwards.

Later on, when you perhaps have no one on the ground, you should be prepared to apply a little extra pressure with your lower leg on the inside if the quarters start to swing this way.

Facing a fence

It may also help, at the very beginning, if the horse seems confused, to ask for the rein-back whilst facing a fence. In this way, he cannot go forward, so it is perhaps more obvious that you are asking him to move back.

More advanced rein-backs

Once you and your horse are completely au fait and relaxed about the rein-back, you may start to think about using it as a real benefit to the training.

Figure 13.5 Rein-back

Here I am in rein-back on my mare Lucy. My upper body is inclined forward, taking the weight off the back of the saddle, to allow the horse's back to rise during the backward steps. I'm supporting my torso upwards so as not to put weight onto the forehand. My lower leg is back, which excites the correct intercostal nerves for backward movement, as in Figure 13.2. Lucy is stepping back correctly in diagonal pairs. Note the very light contact with the rein. No pulling is necessary, and contact can be virtually zero when the horse understands the correct body aids. Photo by Horsepix.

I am not in favour of long rein-backs, involving many strides of backward steps. This is not only too strenuous but also usually causes the horse to hollow the back as the strain is too much.

I would never ask for more than three good diagonal strides back, followed immediately by forward movement. If the horse has moved back correctly, he will have lifted his forehand and taken some weight back onto the haunches. If you don't move forward fairly soon after coming to a halt after the backward steps, you will lose the backward shift of weight. If you move forward straight away (but not so abruptly as to be a rebuke), your horse will move forward with much more collection. In this way, the rein-back can be used as a sort of 'launch-pad' for forward movement in collection. It can be invaluable when asking for extreme collection, and it is one of the ways in which the masters, for instance, General Decarpentry, teach the piaffe. You may not want to reach these dizzy heights of equestrianism, but it helps to understand the principle.

Even in advanced training, the rein-back should still not be practised too often.

Rein-back as an evasion

It is important to be aware that rein-back can be used as an evasion. Sometimes horses will move backwards to avoid something they don't want to do, or are frightened of, such as a jump or a scary object. This is something we must try to avoid at all costs. It can be very dangerous; the horse could back into something or even fall over backwards if it should lead to a rear. The need to follow the forward impulsion aid should be impressed upon the horse.

Clearly, too much reining-back in the school could induce a scenario whereby the horse realises that he can take control by backing-up, and being soured by being asked to do it too much could well be a contributory cause.

If your horse does have a tendency to move backwards when he is scared, I would implore you to leave rein-back well alone until he is very advanced and obedient in his training.

If you do find yourself in the unfortunate situation of a backing-up horse (which you think could end in a rear), perhaps on the road, then a good plan which sometimes works is to try to turn the horse onto a circle. At least then he is moving forward. If he is frightened of going past something scary, then sometimes just allowing him to stand still for some time will work until he tires of that and is happy to move forward. If all else fails, then it is best to dismount. This is not admitting defeat, it is just being sensible. Turning round and going back the way you came may seem also like 'the horse has won', but if he is genuinely scared, then you are both in danger, and discretion is the better part of valour. You can work on giving him confidence in other ways rather than choosing a fight you are never likely to win. Don't worry about what anyone else thinks; your and your horse's safety are more important.

Having said all this, rein-back can be very beneficial and a wonderful tool in our armoury of classical exercises, contributing towards strength, flexibility, collection and obedience.

References

Ref: 13.1 – 'The Classical Seat – The Key to Great Riding' (Paperback) – Loch, Sylvia – Horse & Rider Publication – 2011.

Ref: 13.2 – 'Exercise School for Horse and Rider' – Skipper, Lesley – New Holland Publishers (UK) Ltd. – 2008.

Collection and the beginnings of self-carriage

14

Including tracking-up

Tracking-up

I have mentioned this subject before, but I do not want people to become too concerned with it. Some trainers seem almost obsessed by it to the detriment of the correct training.

The horse's ability to track-up (hind feet falling into the prints of the front feet) will naturally improve as his training progresses. He may begin to over-track, that is, his hind footprints reaching farther forward than his front, but this all depends upon his conformation.

Conformation plays a huge part in the horse's ability to track-up (as well as strength and stage of training), and a horse who does not track-up is not necessarily unable to collect.

Tracking-up should not be sought at the beginning of any lesson. It is always a good idea to allow the horse time to warm up. Even a jog trot, especially in cold weather, at the beginning of a lesson is a good way for horses to warm up before being asked to move forward in a more energetic way.

Generally, the aim of most trainers, riders or handlers is to encourage the horse to 'track-up', but is this really always absolutely necessary? In my opinion it is not. Like most things in classical training, it has to be worked on, and time must be allowed for the necessary strength to be built up.

The horse's ability to track-up is not only dependent on strength and stage of training but very much upon conformation. Some horses will track-up

DOI: 10.1201/9781003503422-15

naturally when they are not really strong nor advanced, whilst others, because of their conformation, may never track-up to the same degree. This does not mean that the latter cannot be trained to a high standard, and they are likely to still be able to collect very well.

The young or green horse

When first coming into work, the green horse will probably not naturally track-up because his hindquarters and back are not sufficiently developed and strong. This also depends on conformation and breed. Many young horses may well track-up easily in walk but fail to do so in the trot. When they are pushed into an extended trot, then tracking-up or even over-tracking may take place, but at what cost? If the extension of the trot is a natural one, say on the lunge, then this may be perfectly okay, but far too often they are pushed forward faster than is comfortable, for far too long a period, in an attempt to create this illusive tracking-up. Quite often it can have the opposite effect, in that being pushed on at a faster pace merely makes the horse rush round with more weight falling onto the forehand and the hind

Figure 14.1 Early Training

Here we see my mare Secret very soon after backing. She is needing light support from the reins and is not tracking-up. Nevertheless, this is a very nice walk for early training. Photo by John Wilson.

legs trailing further behind. This has a detrimental effect on the forehand, possibly damaging/stressing the joints, and is of no true training value to the horse. It is far better to concentrate on working the horse at a steady pace and encouraging the horse to be 'straight' and in a regular rhythm.

Here is Col. Podhajsky's advice on preparing the young horse (Ref: 14.1):

> The first step in preparing the young horse to become a school horse is to develop the hindquarters so that their carrying power exceeds their pushing power. If the hind leg of the horse is to carry the same weight as the foreleg of the corresponding diagonal, it must be placed in the hoof print made by the foreleg, which is below the centre of the gravity, at the exact moment that the other diagonal leaves the ground. The horse can only develop good paces, in full balance when the hind legs track up to the forelegs. Horses with normal conformation will find little difficulty in doing this, but a horse with a weak or lowered back or with weak hindquarters will have much greater difficulty in bringing the hind legs under the body. This fact must be taken into consideration when training and the work must be made easier for such horses.

As we can see, good tracking-up is definitely something to aim for in training, but, like most other things, it should not be hurried and is not essential in all cases, all of the time. Too much attention is often given to it. Each horse is an individual, and his training must respect this.

There are times when even the fully trained horse does not need to be tracking-up. For instance, when warming up, it is quite admissible for him to be allowed to under-track. Once fully warmed up and supple, he can then be encouraged to track-up fully. When performing advanced trot movements such as piaffe, the horse obviously will not track-up.

Straightness

A fact which is sometimes overlooked is that the horse needs to be straight in order for the hind feet to follow the tracks of the forefeet. When on a circle, the horse is said to be straight when he has an even bend commensurate with the size of the circle; his hind feet follow the tracks of the forefeet, and his neck is bent to the same degree as his body. This is regardless of whether he is tracking-up, over-tracking or under-tracking.

It is quite common for a young or green horse, providing he is naturally balanced, to be straight on the lunge or during in-hand work, but once mounted, the hind feet footfalls no longer follow the tracks of the forefeet but step to the side. This crookedness will cause an uneven contact with the bit. This is often caused by the young horse gravitating towards the wall of the arena (if ridden on the track) for support, and since the forehand is narrower than the quarters, the horse therefore becomes crooked. The forehand must be brought away from the wall in order to allow room for the shoulders to be in front of the hindquarters; hence the horse will be made straight again. The horse may also become crooked because of the unaccustomed weight of the rider on his back, which means he has to find a new balance, and being unbalanced can make him crooked. This must be borne in mind, and time and patience must be spent in giving the horse time to adjust, whilst at the same time assisting him by correcting his crookedness.

Good tracking-up is a natural occurrence once the horse is sufficiently supple and strong, providing his conformation allows.

All in all, tracking-up is important, and time must be given for it to develop through correct training; it cannot be hurried. Like everything else, it can never be forced, and too much emphasis should not be placed upon it.

Collection

One of the most important aims of training, after making the horse straight, balanced, relaxed and forward going with good impulsion, is to teach him to collect. Here is a quote from *The Complete Training of Horse and Rider* by Col. Alois Podhajsky (Ref: 14.1):

> The horse in collection must step with his hind legs well under his body, which can be recognised by the fact that the tracks of the hind feet come into or in front of those of the forefeet. This will make the horse arch his back correctly and carry his head higher, thus becoming shorter in his body. . . . Collection is necessary for advanced training as it makes the hindquarters carry a great proportion of the weight and thus relieves the forehand. In this way it will also prevent the horse from wearing out his forelegs prematurely. Correct collection will be possible only when the horse is straight, balanced, and in contact with the bit.
>
> Collection must be obtained by pushing the hindquarters towards the reins, which remain applied. The compression (shortening) of the horse must be produced by pushing forward from behind and not by pulling back with the reins. The latter would create an incorrect collection and the hind feet of the horse would not track up to the

forefeet. Only when the collection is obtained from rear to front will the horse step under the body with his hind legs in such a way that the rider can feel it in the reins. This is called 'the horse steps into the rein.

I believe what Podhajsky is referring to when he says the hind legs should step well under his body is the initial training of collection, not really more advanced collection.

We must bear in mind that in advanced collection, the horse will not track-up at all. He will take shorter steps, and there will be more flexion in the joints of the hind legs. If you think of the advanced collection of piaffe and passage, it is easy to see that it would be impossible for the horse to track-up; more weight is taken back onto the haunches than in any other trot work, but the steps are very much shortened, with the legs lifted higher and greater flexion of the joints. The centre of gravity is taken backwards, so the hind legs are there to support this. Conversely, in extended trot, then the horse will take longer strides and will track-up or over-track.

All the great masters agree that none of this can happen until the horse is strong and supple enough to allow for the extra flexion and weight carrying of the joints of the hind legs the back must also be strong and supple enough to allow for the arching of the back. The trainer/rider must allow enough time for this process without straining the horse.

A common misunderstanding – deep work

One of the most common mistakes made by modern trainers is to try to encourage good hind leg engagement (leg stepping forward under the body) by working the horse in a 'low outline'. Whilst it is true that working in a low or deep outline will help to build up the correct muscles in the back, the practice of forcing the head and neck downwards, especially for lengthy periods, can be exceedingly damaging and has the opposite effect in that it prevents the hind legs from stepping further under the body. Here, again, is what Podhajsky says on the matter (Re: 14.1):

> As already explained, it is of great advantage when breaking in young horses to allow them to seek the contact with a lowered head and, from contact obtained in this manner, to proceed gradually to a correct position.

I think the key word here is to 'allow' the horse to seek the contact with a lowered head, obviously until he is ready to do otherwise.

From everything I have written thus far, you will know that collection is the gathering of the horse with weight being taken back onto the hindquarters, lightening the forehand. It is clear that this cannot be hurried nor forced. When the horse is collected, his gait will be slower, but with greater impulsion, his feet will lift higher from the ground, and his forehand will be lighter.

Before he can collect, he needs to be 'dressage straight', that is as near as possible, equally bent in each direction on a bend and straight on a straight line.

All the exercises described so far are designed to gradually build up collection by building the strength and flexibility of the back, quarters and hind leg joints.

In the early stages, it can be helpful to allow the horse to work with a low head and neck outline for short periods. This can help to build up the back muscles, but on no account, as mentioned previously, should this ever be forced. If the head and neck are forced down, it has a detrimental effect of stiffening the very muscles you are trying to strengthen, and it can do a great deal of harm to the muscles around the withers as well as the back.

Here's what Lesley Skipper, in her book *Exercise School for Horses*, says about deep work, which is actually quite a complicated subject and should never be confused with rollkur or hyperflexion of the head and neck (Ref: 14.2):

> Deep work involves working the horse with his head and neck lowered, his topline rounded and his hindquarters engaged. It can be carried out on the lunge or under saddle. It is often confused with 'long and low', but the latter does not necessarily involve rounding of the topline and is mainly used for relaxation, whereas true deep work really makes the horse's muscles work.

Lesley goes on to describe the physiological benefits, but then goes on to say the following:

> Still, this work does have its drawbacks. If the work is carried out with the horse's topline overstretched, this can result in damage to the supraspinous ligament and even to the spine itself. On the other hand, if the horse's hindquarters are not engaged, the topline will not be stretched and the horse will simply fall onto his forehand, increasing stress on the already vulnerable forelimbs. This is why deep work is best introduced on the lunge, while the horse is free from the weight of a rider and where hindquarters can be observed to ensure they are

active enough. Whether on the lunge or under saddle, this work must not be carried out too frequently or prolonged for more than about ten minutes on each rein (it would be best to work up to this gradually).

My own experience of deep work is that not all horses take to it at all, and this is where the temptation to use gadgets to 'show them the way' comes in. Some of these gadgets are not too extreme, but others are lethal. I feel that it is so easy to do damage to a horse in this way that it is best to be guided by the horse. If he is happy to lower his head and round his back, then by all means, allow or encourage this for a short time. At the very least, he should always be allowed a break from work to walk and stretch on a long rein. Provided he is allowed to do this frequently, I don't think you can go far wrong. But true deep work is perhaps best left to the masters, or the horse himself!

The 'engagement' or 'reach' of the hind legs

Many trainers, including myself, often use the word 'engagement' when referring to the hind legs reaching further forward under the horse's body. Since engagement can have other meanings, such as flexion of the hocks, stifles and hips, perhaps the words 'hind leg reach' would be more appropriate.

Hind leg reach is most desirable as the horse progresses as it means he is really building up strength in the back, quarters and hind limbs, but it must be done as a natural progression through the classical training exercises. As I keep reiterating (but make no apology for doing so), It should *never* be attempted by mechanical means, such as lunging equipment designed to 'compress' the horse's body (such as ropes and pulleys encompassing the horse) and force the hind legs forward. This can only cause harm, which may be long lasting. One can only imagine the strain on the back, particularly, that this must cause.

All the exercises we have covered so far have been with a view to building the horse up for collection.

Shoulder-in, after leg-yield and shoulder-fore, is perhaps the only lateral exercise you can begin before good collection is achieved. This is providing you only practise one or two steps at a time in walk at first. This will help the horse to collect, but bear in mind that he will not be capable of a good shoulder-in until he has attained collection; starting very gradually and gently does help to build strength and suppleness towards this goal.

Figure 14.2 Good Reach

Here you can see Secret with good reach with both front and hind legs in trot. Whether she is tracking-up or not is less important than the symmetry of the front and hind reach. In trot, the cannon bones of the outside hind and inside forelegs are at the same angle to the ground: parallel. This then gives the legs the appearance of forming, what we call in dressage terms, perfect 'A's front and back, which is very desirable. Photo by Lesley Skipper.

Collection is required for a really good shoulder-in, and shoulder-in itself builds up this collection.

All lateral exercises rely heavily on the horse's ability to 'reach', push and take weight with a particular hind leg. Obviously, the advanced exercises should not be attempted until the horse can collect correctly. They all work on the basis of loading one leg at a time and building up the pushing power of another hind leg, so they must be practised equally on both reins.

In ordinary walk and trot work, you should experience moments of lightness in your hand, with the horse much lighter in the shoulders. This feeling is usually just fleeting to begin with, but it will grow as time goes on.

Defining the terms and understanding the leg movements

All this may make the onlooker think that the 'reach' of the hind legs is of utmost importance in collection, but this is most definitely not so, other

Figure 14.3 Beginning to Arch Neck

Here we see Secret with an arched neck and a moment of self-carriage. Shortly after this, she was asked to move forward again in a longer trot with more support from the reins. This is because she was not ready to sustain this amount of collection for too long at that time. Note how the trot is shortened, with higher steps and less reach. Photo by Lesley Skipper.

than in lateral work. I quote from Paul Belasik's book *A Search for Collection* (Ref: 14.3):

> Collection is synonymous with the ability to lift easily or, as we often say today, carry. This carrying involves the back, abdomen, psoas, etc. I think many people use the terms 'collection', engagement and 'flexion' interchangeably, and this is confusing. Some writer/trainers will refer to engagement as being the protraction of the hind leg. More engagement here means reach under the body. We know now from current biomechanics that collection occurs when there is a shorter protraction and retraction; a shorter stroke of the hind legs.

Paul goes on to say the following:

> As de la Guérinière so carefully described, you cannot assume that increased flexion or engagement is synonymous with collection. Many pressed horses will show more and more flexion in the hind limb joints, but if this increased activity is a result of leaning on the reins attached to the pillars or the rider's hands, or if it becomes so active

Figure 14.4 Piaffe

Here we see Sylvia Loch on her late Iberian stallion Espada performing an exemplary piaffe. You can easily see how the hind legs do not reach so far forward in this highly collected movement. The weight is taken back on the haunches, and the hind legs are there to support it. Therefore, tracking-up would be impossible. Photo courtesy of Sylvia Loch

that the horse supports it by balancing on his forelegs, it becomes the opposite of collection, which is the ability to lift the forehand. A sleepy horse may be asked for more engagement, which could lead to better collection, but if the engagement becomes excessive it will move away from collection to a balance on the forehand. So, engagement is not synonymous with collection.

Personally, I don't think we actually need current biomechanics to teach us that more 'reach' with the hind legs means more collection. We only need to look at a horse performing, say, the piaffe and then moving into extended trot. We can easily see that the hind legs in the piaffe, whilst not 'camped out behind', are not reaching forward under the belly. The weight is taken back onto the haunches, and the hind legs are there to support it.

When the horse moves forward from this excellent 'launch pad' of the piaffe, with much weight on the haunches, and extends the trot, the reach of the hind legs is profound. He is using the strength and weight accumulated in the haunches to push forward and extend.

You can also see that if the hind legs were this far under the belly in piaffe, he would fall over backwards!

How and when to ask for collection on a straight line

We can ask for more collection in trot by using temporary 'closing aids' to slow the speed down, whilst still keeping our lower legs intermittently asking for impulsion. The best impulsion aids are usually very fast, exciting (not hard) touches with the lower leg. I find that asking in trot to begin with is easier than in walk, probably because the horse usually has more impulsion naturally, but many people prefer to begin at the walk.

As we well know, you cannot and should not try to obtain collection by the reins. The energy has to come from behind the saddle and then be contained by the holding body aids, with the merest backup by gentle restraint in the reins.

When the horse is in an energetic but not fast trot, start by using some of your half-halt body aids: lift your upper torso, imagine yourself growing in height and slightly close your upper inner thighs to arrest some of the forward motion (but not so much as the horse thinks he has to stop). Advance your waist towards your hands, and have a feeling of lightening the back of your seat, putting more weight down the front of the saddle.

When the horse feels and responds to the arresting aids, excite the impulsion by discreet taps with your lower legs, very slightly back from the 'on the girth' position but not so far back as the rein-back position.

You can discourage a faster pace by gently 'feeling' with the reins, but do not attempt to restrict the horse's head too much. If he responds to these aids, give with the rein.

You should gradually begin to feel the beginning of collection as the horse lightens the forehand and transfers a little weight backwards. He will probably still need a definite connection from your hand to the bit, albeit very gentle.

To begin with, this collection should only be ridden for a few strides, and then the rider should release the horse with the knees and thighs and slightly open the fingers on the reins, allowing the horse to move more forward.

This can be practised by intertwining lateral exercises with upward and downward transitions, for example, halt to working trot, then collect a few strides, back to working trot, back to walk and stretch and relax. Canter transitions can also be used to build up strength, balance and add variety.

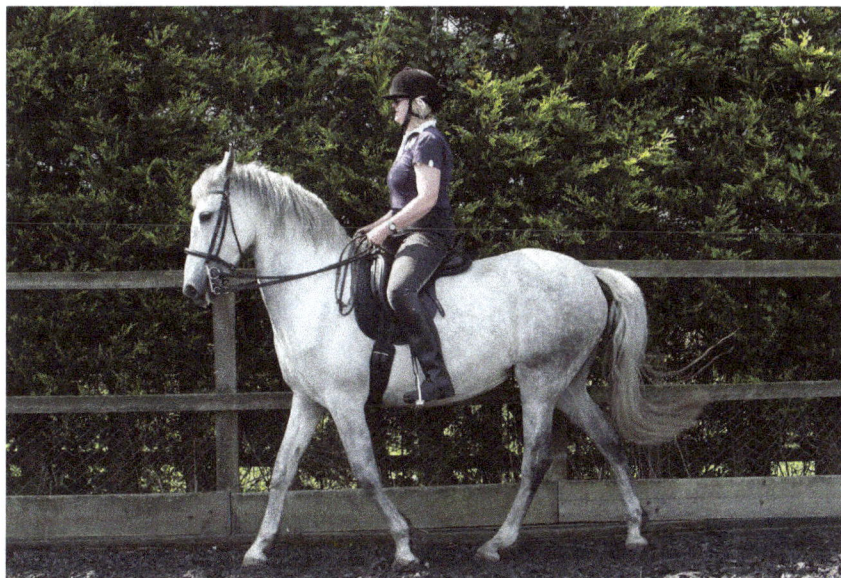

Figure 14.5 Beginnings of Collection

Here we see a moment of early collection and the effort that Secret is giving in order to collect and take weight off the forehand. As soon as she gives this for a few seconds, I ask for a longer trot as she shouldn't be pushed into performing this for too long in these early stages. Note how the reach is less far forward than in Figure 14.2, due to a degree of collection, but the legs still show an 'A' shape, just at a more closed angle. Photo by Lesley Skipper.

Self-carriage

In this way, the horse will become more and more physically able to collect and more than likely very willing to enjoy the experience again.

Gradually the feeling of lightness on the rein will naturally be felt. When the horse is fairly confident in his collection, the rider can give with the rein for a couple of strides, whilst retaining the other collection aids of torso and legs. If the horse remains in the same frame, then this is proof of his self-carriage in collection (see Figures 14.3 and 14.5), but he may not be able to remain in this self-carriage for too long in the beginning; everything takes time to build up, but what a wonderful journey it all is!

Don't try too many times in any one schooling session. Over the weeks and months, you should find that the horse understands your aids immediately and can comply for a little longer. With time and patience, the horse will come temporarily into self-carriage. He will begin to arch his neck upwards as he takes weight back, with virtually no contact with the reins (see Figures 14.3 and 14.5).

Don't be too greedy and expect this collection and self-carriage to last; it is quite strenuous. But if you attain a few strides, you should be very pleased and again go forward into a longer trot; then give the horse a break and walk on a long rein.

As time goes on, you can ask for this collection more frequently, not only on the track but sometimes on a circle, just to add a little variety to the work. In effect, what you are doing is shortening and then lengthening the strides (not asking for actual extension), building up strength and flexibility.

Lightness in the hand

False lightness can occur when a severe bit is used. The horse does not want to touch the bit, and the feeling therefore in the rider's hands is one of lightness, but this does not necessarily go hand in hand with the transference of weight behind, or true lightness. The horse will have a hollow back, and there will be no feeling of weight transferring to the quarters. Sylvia Loch's book *Dressage in Lightness* contains some very illuminating diagrams showing exactly this (Ref: 14.4).

The horse may go above or behind the bit to avoid the contact. In classical riding, we aim for a gentle acceptance of the bit.

We must not 'throw away' the contact with the horse's mouth until he is ready for self-carriage. Just give the rein when you feel he is carrying himself, then support him again when he begins to lose that feeling.

The horse is normally gently on the bit with a sensitive contact from the rein when in collection. You will feel when he can move in self-carriage and no longer needs the support of your hands.

References

Ref: 14.1 – 'The Complete Training of Horse and Rider' – Podhajsky, Col. Alois – Translated by Eva Podhajsky & Col. V.D.S. Williams – Harrap – 1967.

Ref: 14.2 – 'Exercise School for Horse and Rider' – Skipper, Lesley – New Holland Publishers (UK) Ltd. – 2008.

Ref: 14.3 – 'A Search for Collection – Science and Art in Riding' – Belasik, Paul – J.A. Allen – 2009.

Ref: 14.4 – 'Dressage in Lightness – Speaking the Horse's Language' – Loch, Sylvia – J.A. Allen – 2000.

Lengthening and extension

15

Including trotting poles and transitions building up to extension

Trotting poles

Although not an absolute essential, trotting poles can be a good way to introduce the horse to lengthened strides. They can also help to encourage the horse to lower his head, round his back and build up back muscles. It is best to introduce them when the horse is on the lunge. Then, later on, they can be used in ridden work.

The horse will usually lower his head whilst going over the poles, then lift back up to his normal position afterwards. This is a good thing and, as we have noted before, the horse should never be forced with gadgets, nor by the rider's hands.

When riding over trotting poles, you should use rising trot and give with the reins as you go over the poles, allowing the horse to stretch out and down as he wishes. It can be helpful also to teach both horse and rider co-ordination, rhythm and judgement/adjustment of strides.

I would suggest, if the horse has never been over poles before, to just use one pole on the ground placed, say, on the track in the middle of the long side of the school. Let the horse see the pole first, perhaps walk around it at first and then calmly walk over it. Once he is perfectly happy about this, you can introduce another pole. Stay in walk, and let him work out his striding over the two poles. He will probably find it a little difficult at first, but just let

DOI: 10.1201/9781003503422-16

Figure 15.1 Trotting Poles

Arabian stallion Nivalis (owned by Brian Skipper), relaxed and happy, negotiating trotting poles whilst being loose schooled. Photo by Lesley Skipper.

him take his time, encouraging him gently onwards. You can do this either in hand or under saddle. Some horses find it reassuring if the handler actually walks over the poles with them to begin with.

As these lessons progress, you can add another pole, gradually building up to four poles. Be mindful of the fact that using two poles may encourage the horse to jump over them. If you find this to be the case, then proceed from one pole to three.

Here is a rough guide as to distancing of the poles:

Trotting Poles

Ponies – 1.2–1.3 m (4–4.5 ft) apart
Horses – 1.3–1.4 m (4.5–5 ft) apart

Walking Poles

Horses and Ponies – 2.7 m (9 ft) apart

These are just approximate distances as horses' strides can vary immensely. You're fairly safe with the 9 ft distance apart in walk for both horses and ponies, but when it comes to the trot, you need to check the suitable distance, preferably on the lunge. The horse's footfalls should land in between, roughly equidistant of the two poles. If they land immediately in front of, or immediately behind the next pole, then the spacing is incorrect.

Trotting pole work is great for building up strength, agility, balance and rhythm. It should never be ridden in sitting trot.

It is always very helpful, if at all possible, when using trotting poles to have a helper on hand to replace the poles as they are bound to be knocked out of position occasionally, especially at first when the horse is learning how to judge the stride and rhythm. From this point of view, it may be better, if no helper is available, to work the horse on the lunge as you can then stop and re-adjust the poles without dismounting and mounting.

In many ways, my own personal preference is to use trotting poles on the lunge. You can then see exactly how your horse is using himself, and he has freedom to use the poles to optimal advantage.

When the horse is very relaxed and using the poles easily, with feet landing equidistant in between the poles, you can try to encourage a lengthened stride by slightly increasing the distance between the poles. This is much easier to do, and to see what is happening, with the horse on the lunge.

Canter Poles

Horses – 2.7–3.7 m (9–12 ft) apart

This is obviously a very rough guide, and I do not think that cantering over poles (apart from the odd placing pole before a jump) is particularly helpful.

Lengthening

Lengthening of strides in all gaits can be practised throughout training, but I would not recommend this until the horse is well balanced and moving forward easily from the aids – relaxed, rhythmic and straight with impulsion.

Different stages of lengthening

Within the dressage test system, there are various degrees of lengthened strides which are recognised and required in dressage tests. They are mentioned elsewhere in this book in the appropriate chapters, but for ease of reference, here is a summary, in order of length of stride.

Walk

Collected walk	shortest, most elevated strides
Medium walk	Normal or natural walk, longer strides than in collection and the one mostly used in training
Extended walk	Longer strides than in medium

Figure 15.2 Good Lengthening

Sylvia Loch with her Lusitano stallion Prazer, being asked for fairly advanced lengthening (but not actual extension), which he does easily and correctly, with good hind and foreleg reach. Photo by Lesley Skipper.

Trot

Collected trot	Shortest, most elevated strides
Working trot	Normal or natural strides, longer than in collection and the one mostly used in training
Medium trot	Longer strides than working trot, but not as long as extended
Extended trot	Ultimate length of stride in trot

Canter

Collected canter	Shortest, most elevated strides
Working canter	Normal or natural canter, longer strides than in collection and the one mostly used in training
Medium canter	Longer strides than working canter but not as long as extended
Extended canter	Ultimate length of stride in canter, without breaking into gallop

Full extension in any gait should never be requested until the horse's collection is well established.

I think the best gait in which to begin teaching the horse to lengthen the stride is the trot. As mentioned before, attempting to alter the walk stride too soon can really ruin the rhythm of the walk. Lengthening in canter is quite an advanced exercise and best left until the horse is fairly well advanced. It's much better to use the walk/trot/canter transitions to confirm a really well-balanced canter in a steady pace. The horse can be easily pushed out of balance if asked to lengthen in canter too soon in the school. Of course, whilst out hacking, the horse may well lengthen the canter stride on a straight line, and this is fine, but it is totally different when asking for this in the school.

Therefore, the trot, which is, in any case, the mainstay gait of training, is the obvious gait in which to begin to ask for lengthened strides.

Before asking for lengthening, you should have begun to help the horse to take a little weight back onto the haunches, via such exercises as turn on the haunches, demi-pirouette and others. Since the horse cannot extend correctly until he can collect, all we are asking to begin with is merely a suggestion of a longer stride, and this must not be over-ridden. If we do this tactfully now and, after the lengthened strides, ask him to come back to a normal stride, this will help his balance and will hopefully give him a slight feeling of collection when coming back to a shorter stride.

Here is what Sylvia Loch has to say in her book *Dressage in Lightness*, published by J.A. Allen (Ref: 15.1):

> Remember, at this stage (novice) we are not looking either for collection or for extended strides – these will develop later. What we do want to show to our horse is that he is quite capable of offering us two contrasting trots – one more open and forward, the other more rounded and contained. Both of them will require concentration and activity behind.

Even when we are not asking for true extension, it is imperative to understand the important classical principles of extension and to know exactly what to aim for and what to avoid.

First steps of lengthening

So far in the horse's training, our concentration has been on encouraging the horse to be forward, rhythmic and balanced. Nothing is going to change;

as mentioned previously, the rhythm should remain the same – we are just asking for a longer stride.

Start with your horse in a normal, active trot down the long side of the arena; shortly after coming round the corner from the short side, take your lower legs slightly forward, and give a gentle forward aid with your inner calves in this spot (button C to stimulate the muscles which extend the foreleg; see Chapter 13). At the same time, take your shoulders very slightly back. This will have the effect of putting more weight on the back of your seat-bones than is normal in the upright classical position. Just this slight adjustment of position is enough to cause a driving effect on the horse's back. There is no need for any exaggerated leaning back or pushing with the seat. (Do not continue this position for too long.) At the same moment, you need to give with your hands slightly to allow/encourage the horse to move his head and neck forward and outwards, but don't abandon the horse's mouth. You don't want the horse to suddenly thrust forward onto the forehand. On the contrary, you are aiming for more engagement with the hindquarters. These aids should be applied very gently and modestly, and if the horse responds, that is, you can feel a slight difference in his stride, then normalise your position after about two or three strides, and ask him to return to his normal trot. Make much of him; let him know you are really pleased, and try again on the other rein.

Never overdo these first attempts, and especially do not ask for too many lengthened strides at first as you will probably only succeed in pushing him downhill onto the forehand as he struggles to do as you ask.

Take plenty of breaks

If you don't seem to get much response at first, don't worry, just try again, possibly giving your forward leg aids a little firmer (i.e., a firmer nudge).

Always ride lengthened strides in rising trot during the training process. Then, when your horse is strong and well balanced enough, you can begin some sitting trot. So, use sitting trot in the approach, then go rising when asking for lengthening; come back to sitting when you neutralise your aids, and ask the horse to cease lengthening and come back to a normal trot.

Some horses, usually those with upright shoulder conformation, find lengthening more difficult, so don't expect too much too soon. In fact, a lengthened stride for an upright shouldered horse would look quite different to one whose shoulder is more sloping. This is of no consequence and should not be penalised in the competition arena. The horse should be judged on the amount of lengthening of which his conformation allows rather than a 'showy' leg thrust, which is more akin to a bad circus act. You should be able to just feel a difference in the stride – it does not have to be great – with an increased push from behind, which can also be felt by the rider.

When your horse becomes more familiar with these two contrasting trots practised on a straight line, we can begin to introduce the same thing on a circle, but only a few strides at first.

This may also be a good time to introduce the horse to more transitions in general, such as walk to halt, progressing to halt to trot. It may be very helpful to use the halt to trot in preparation for the contained trot, prior to asking for a lengthened one. In this way, the horse is more 'together' and on the aids before he is asked to do something more difficult.

However, do not demand trot to halt transitions at the novice stage; this is far more challenging to the novice horse and requires more strength behind than he is likely to have developed as yet. As in all things, don't overdo the transitions. Too many halts can be seen as a punishment to the horse. So, all things in moderation, and listen to your horse; try to feel what he is feeling and thinking. Be generous with your praise and refrain from too much criticism, assuming that most faults are probably your own anyway! We all make mistakes, so be patient with your horse and yourself. In this way, you will progress gradually, with enjoyment for both parties.

Extension

Good extension

Never attempt extension until the horse is well established in collection.

True extension can only come from collection, and the horse has to be in a degree of collection, even during extension. His hindquarters must be carrying a good degree of the weight as he pushes forward from his hind legs, allowing his whole frame to elongate and forelegs to reach out. But the forelegs should not reach out to such a degree that the feet land heel first (this is very damaging to the tendons and other parts of the forelegs). Obviously, the centre of gravity moves slightly forward as compared to, say, the piaffe. This is borne out by the placement of the hind legs reaching well under the belly, which is the centre of gravity, whereas, as mentioned before, the hind legs in the piaffe remain underneath the haunches to support the centre of gravity there. Nevertheless, during extension, there should still be collection, otherwise the weight will be thrown badly onto the forehand.

Extension means exactly that: the whole frame of the horse extends to execute a longer stride. This does not mean faster. Although, of course, more ground will be covered quicker, the rhythm of the footfalls should remain the same. The hind legs should come forward and under the belly in synchronisation with the forelegs moving forward. The head and neck stretch forward as the hindquarters make a forward thrust, with deeper reach or engagement of the hind end.

Things to avoid in extension

It is a very bad fault when the hindquarters are not engaged and the hind legs lose synchronisation with the forelimbs. It is a sad fact that this happens in many competitions, and people are fooled and impressed by exaggerated thrusting with the forelegs. This can happen when the horse is pushed too hard by a harsh driving seat, pushing the front end forward, then the reins are applied which forces the forelegs upwards. This is what causes the all

Figure 15.3 Good Extension

Lola Saville on her horse Petra in a very good extension for a young horse and rider. The rider is sitting in a lovely upright classical position, not leaning back, and the horse is extending well from behind as well as in front. For perfection, the head and neck could be given a little more rein for further extension, which should prevent the toe flicking, but on the whole, this is excellent, with the horse's nose nicely just in front of the vertical. Photo courtesy of Lola Saville.

Figure 15.4 Bad Extension

Here we see the rider leaning back, pushing the horse forward with weight on the back of the saddle which flattens the horse's back, whilst at the same time driving with the lower legs and restricting the horse by a tight hold on the reins. The horse is unable to extend at all behind the saddle, hence the hind legs are trailing. The front legs are forced to 'flick' forward. Photo by Lesley Skipper.

too often seen toe flicking, which is very detrimental to the longevity of the horse's limbs. It is an extremely bad fault and definitely not classical. A good dressage judge will penalise this rather than reward it, but it would definitely help if the spectating public could understand how bad it is and feel shocked instead of impressed.

Here is what Paul Belasik says on the subject, in his book *Dressage for the 21st Century* (Ref: 15.2):

> Obviously, different horses will have different sizes of extended trot. The extended trot should show nearly equal activity of the hind and forelegs. The cannon bones should be approximately parallel when in full extension. If the fore cannon is angled at 45 degrees to the ground, the opposite hind cannon should show a similar angle. Extended trots that show dramatic reach with the foreleg, but an unmatched hind leg with half the reach, have to be considered faulty. Too much disparity will demand that the horse hollow its back as in the Spanish walk, which is not the aim of the powerful, gymnastic, extended trot. When

executed correctly, the extended trot shows the maximum of swing, elasticity and strength. It should never appear restrained, tight or false in any way.

It is important to remember what Paul says here – "different horses have different sizes of extended trot". Conformation plays a big part in the appearance of the extension. Horses with relatively upright shoulders will not display such a big reach forward with their forelegs, but this does not mean that their extension is any less good or correct – just less spectacular. Warmbloods have been chosen for some years now for their conformational ability to extend often to an exaggerated degree. They usually find it more difficult to perform a good passage/piaffe. On the other hand, the Iberian breeds, who find collection much easier, do not usually display the same type of spectacular extension. Nevertheless, the extensions they display can be very correct and beautiful. Extension is all about extending the whole frame, not merely the forelegs.

How to ride a good extension

The best way to begin asking for extension is from a good collected trot. It can be built up gradually from normal lengthened strides just by asking for longer strides.

The aids are the same as for lengthening, but the rider just asks a little more to begin with. At this stage, we can begin to use our impulsion aid, more specifically, just in front of the 'on the girth' position – button 'C', as described in Chapter 13. As you know, this excites the nerves, which stimulates the forward thrust of the forelegs.

Don't try to drive too hard with your seat by leaning back, as is often seen in competition. This is wrong and damaging to the horse's back and can cause the back to hollow – the very opposite of what you want. To encourage the horse forward with your seat, you only need to take your shoulders back slightly, which will cause more weight to fall to the back of the saddle, and act as a driving aid, but don't overdo or prolong this action. Once the horse is extending, resume your normal upright position.

When first asking for extension, as when merely lengthening, just ask for a few strides at a time, then come back to collection; then give your horse a rest, and walk on a long rein.

As these lessons progress, you can begin to ask for more extended strides, but don't ask for too many too soon. If you attain a few good extended strides, it is better to come back to collection. Often the horse cannot sustain a good extension (in the same way as he couldn't sustain collection at first) for too long, and it is better to come back to collection before he starts to fall onto the forehand, having lost the collection from the hindquarters.

One good exercise is to collect the trot, to the highest degree that he is capable, on the short side of the arena. After coming around the second corner of the short side, make the horse straight and ask for extension; come back to collection just after the halfway marker. When you can extend all the way down the long side, make sure you come back to collection well before the corner. Remember to work on both reins.

You can do the same exercise across the diagonal. Collect the trot and turn across the school. Don't begin the extension until he is completely straight, then ask for the extension. How soon you come back to collection will depend not only on how easily he can extend but also his size and how quickly he covers the ground. You can make this exercise more demanding by riding just a few strides in extension after turning off the quarter marker and straightening, then coming back to collection at 'X' in the centre of the school. You will probably find, if your horse is quite large, that you are too near to the next quarter marker to ask for more extension, but you can aim for this as time progresses and more precision is possible.

To build up the collection before attempting extension, it is a good idea to work on more exacting transitions.

Halt to trot

I think it best to begin with halt to trot, as trot to halt is even more strenuous.

You need to attain a good square halt, with the horse standing to attention, ready to move forward, with his quarters well engaged (see Chapter 5 'The halt and half-halt'). Sit very upright in your good, classical seat position; think tall with expanded chest. Give a light but 'electric' tap with your inner calf at the 'on the girth' position, and allow the horse forward with your hands. Don't throw the reins at him, but don't restrain him in any way. As he begins to move forward, give another light tap at the girth, making it clear that you want more than walk.

At first, this will probably be quite a surprise as you have probably only ever asked for trot from walk previously. So, accept a stride or two of walk at first, then trot. Gradually you will be able to attain the trot straight from the halt. Don't hassle the horse; give him time to understand what you want and comply. This may take some weeks, practising just two or three times per schooling session.

Trot to halt

Trot to halt is a good deal more difficult. It requires a good deal of collection and engagement of the hindquarters, with a lightened forehand, to enable the horse to come to a good halt without dropping weight onto the forehand.

Start from as collected a trot as he is capable, though obviously not a fast trot. Sit very tall, and use all the arresting aids described in Chapter 5 for the halt: Close your upper thighs and knees, advance your waist towards your hands and give slight restraining 'feels' on the reins, like squeezing water out of a sponge. Do not lean back, think very tall, and have a feeling of allowing more weight onto the front of your seat, freeing up the back of the saddle.

If you have used these aids for the halt up until now, the horse will readily know what you are requesting, but again, it will be a bit of a shock that you are not just asking him to walk from the trot. At first, he is bound to come back to walk before he halts. This is fine and to be expected. Just gradually work on reducing the number of walk strides before the halt. This can be done over a matter of weeks. It is far better to allow him to walk another stride or two rather than to come to a severe, unbalanced halt.

It is very important that you keep your body tall and upright, with a feeling of helping the horse to keep his forehand upright. Use your lower calf muscles gently against his sides to encourage him to halt with his hind legs underneath his belly. Keep a gentle, supportive feel on the reins, with a feeling of helping him to keep the forehand up, but do not pull.

Once he has mastered the technique of coming to a good halt, with lightness in his forehand, he will be ready to take off again in any gait from the halt.

Halt to canter

Obviously, it takes a good deal more strength and thrust to strike off into canter from the halt than to trot from the halt, but it is the obvious next stage after the halt/trot and trot/halt transitions have been well established.

Much of the same applies to this transition as to halt to trot.

Come to a good square halt in as collected a frame as possible. I suggest you halt on the track of the long side, just after coming around the corner of the short side of the school. It is best to try this first on your horse's preferred strike off rein. Always make things as easy as possible to start with.

Don't sustain the halt for too long, or you may lose the collection. Sit very tall, with expanded chest and change your aids to the canter position, that is, inside leg on the girth and outside leg slightly behind the girth.

Make sure that your inside hip is advanced as this is necessary to give room for the advancement of the horse's inside hip (see Chapter 7, 'The canter'). Try to have the feeling of slightly lightening your seat, especially at the back of the saddle.

In the same way as when asking for the trot from halt, when you accepted a stride or two of walk, likewise, you must expect a couple of trot and/or walk strides before the canter. But gradually, with time and patience, these strides will decrease until you can achieve the strike off from the halt.

If your horse is reluctant, then maybe it is too soon in his training, and he has not yet built up the strength for this transition. In this case, don't worry; just leave it alone for a while, maybe months, before trying again. Never hassle or try to be too forceful; all will come with time and patience.

If you are successful and attain the canter after not too many strides in a slower gait, make much of the horse and give him a break on a long rein.

Canter to halt

As trot to halt is more difficult than halt to trot, so is the canter to halt. It is an extremely strenuous exercise and requires a considerable amount of strength and collection, so don't attempt it until you are sure your horse is ready.

We see so many very bad canter to halt transitions in films, where the rider hauls on the reins whilst leaning back. This causes the horse's back and neck to hollow, and he comes to a painful halt with weight falling badly onto the forelegs. This is extremely damaging. What we are aiming for in the beginning is for the horse to halt in his own time, with his back rounded, hind legs well engaged under his belly and weight taken back onto the haunches with a light forehand. If this means he has to trot before doing so, all well and good. In fact, in the beginning, he is almost bound to do so. This should be allowed. These trot strides can be reduced as time goes on. It is far better to err on the side of caution and allow more time for him to halt rather than insist on a halt which is unbalanced and damaging.

Most of the same principles apply as when halting from the trot – you must keep your upper body tall and think very erect, never leaning back. When you are ready to ask for the transition, neutralise your canter aids, that is, return your outside leg to the 'on the girth' position and close your knees and thighs, keeping your calf muscles very gently against his sides (but without giving impulsion aids) to encourage him to halt in collection.

Use your hands to gently support him in the halt, and reinforce the halting aids, but on no account should you pull on the reins.

It is obviously better to ask for this halt transition from as collected a canter as possible, and don't try after a lengthy time in canter. About six strides of canter is enough before you begin to prepare him for the transition. A gentle half-halt can be used just before you change to neutral aids from your canter position if you find this helps.

Asking for extension from rein-back

Another very good and exciting way of practising the extended trot is to ask for it from rein-back.

In Chapter 13, I described how to move forward in walk from the halt after the rein-back. Before asking for extended trot after rein-back, you should practise ordinary trot from rein-back. Obviously, none of this should be done until you have established halt to trot and trot to halt transitions.

All of these transitions are obviously strenuous and should not be attempted until the horse is fairly advanced in his training.

If your rein-back has been good, meaning your horse is moving smoothly back in diagonal pairs, utilising his back muscles (not hollowing the back) and taking weight back onto the haunches, then you have a perfect 'launch-pad', so to speak, to surge forward into either collected trot, extended trot or even canter.

As soon as the three steps of rein-back have been performed, and you have halted, quickly change your position to that for extended trot. Your legs may move forward to give impulsion at 'button B' just in front of the 'on the girth' position. Your upper torso resumes the upright position, and initially, you may take your shoulders back slightly to indicate to the horse, through the slight push this will cause on your seat, that you wish him to spring forward into extension.

Keep a gentle connection with his mouth, but allow him enough room in the reins to extend his head and neck. Don't throw the reins at him, but at the same time, don't restrain him. Don't lean back – just think tall.

If you have already practised some strides of extension and rein-back to ordinary trot, it will not be too much of a shock to him that you are now asking him to extend from the rein-back. If the rein-back has been successful and carried out well, you will feel a good deal more thrust from the hind legs as all this coiled up energy in his quarters is released forward. As in all exercises, don't ride it too often in any one schooling session, and give your horse a reward by relaxing on a long rein in walk afterwards, giving him much praise – and be pleased with yourself!

References

Ref: 15.1 – 'Dressage in Lightness – Speaking the Horse's Language' – Loch, Sylvia – J.A. Allen – 2000.
Ref: 15.2 – 'Dressage for the 21st Century' – Belasik, Paul – J.A. Allen – 2001.

Counter-canter and flying change

16

Counter-canter

As mentioned before, counter-bend is not at all the same as counter-canter.

I consider counter-canter to be a fairly advanced exercise. Some horses find it relatively easy, but a vast majority struggle with this movement. I would therefore not attempt it until an advanced stage of training has been attained. It should, in any case, never be attempted until the horse can easily perform good collection in canter, which in itself is quite advanced.

If you are on the left rein (travelling anti-clockwise around the school) and ask the horse to counter-counter, you first need to position him to the right, with a definite right flexion but not too much bend. Then you must put yourself into the right canter position, following the rider's aids for the canter, as given in Chapter 7 'The canter', and as follows:
Your right hip should be advanced. Bring your left shoulder slightly forward, look slightly to the right (look where you want the horse to look) and take your left leg and hip back, keeping your right leg under your right hip. You should be looking slightly to the outside of the school.

In this way, the horse should strike off with his left hind, follow it with his right hind and left fore together and, lastly, move his right fore, which will be the leading leg. Everything will be positioned right (as in a right-handed skipping motion), even though you are travelling left. Thought of in this way, you can see that the right-hand side has become the inside of the movement. The horse therefore retains inside bend.

I do not intend to delve into the training of counter-canter in too much depth as it is not something which the more novice horse and rider need to consider just yet. But, having a good knowledge of what it actually consists

DOI: 10.1201/9781003503422-17

Figure 16.1 Counter-Canter

Sylvia Loch on her Lusitano stallion Prazer. The photo and caption are reproduced by kind permission of Sylvia Loch and Kenilworth Press from the book *The Balanced Horse, The Aids by Feel, Not Force*, written by Sylvia Loch and published by and copyright Kenilworth Press.

'Here, I have just asked for counter-canter on the right rein. My right leg has moved back to engage Prazer's right hind for the strike-off, and my weight, gaze and energy is all to the left' (Ref: 16.1). Photo copyright Kenilworth Press.

of and the difference between counter-bending and merely cantering on the wrong leg is very helpful to understand. The subject is covered in much depth in many of the books by the great riding masters. I would particularly recommend a book titled *Masters of Equitation on Counter-Canter and Flying Changes*, compiled by Martin Diggle (Ref: 16.2). In this book, the author gives an insight into the thoughts of many of the masters, with his own interpretation and quotes from the masters. It is a brilliant and convenient way in which to familiarise yourself with some of the works of the best horsemen of all time with helpful guidance of the author.

Ways of teaching counter-canter

Down the long side of the arena

If your horse can canter well, in a balanced and collected stride, and you do want to try counter-canter, the best way to begin asking is down the long side of the arena.

You could start in collected trot. After coming round the second corner of the short side of the arena, straighten the horse, give a gentle half-halt if required, then request an outside flexion, and position yourself for the counter-canter as described earlier. Then ask for the strike off. Make sure you come back to trot well before the corner of the arena. Obviously, you must practise on both reins.

If this has been successful, perhaps a few schooling sessions afterwards, you could begin in true canter. After coming round the second corner of the short side of the school in this canter, come back to trot for a stride or two. Then, reverse the flexion and your canter aids, and ask for a canter on the other leg.

It is important that you come back to trot well before the corner of the school. In this way, you are not asking him to negotiate any bends or corners. This can actually help to confirm the accuracy of your own body aids and sharpen the horse's response.

Theoretically, this may be no different from asking for canter on a specific lead when out hacking on a straight line. However, he may well be confused at first because all through his training up until now, he has learnt the importance of striking off with the correct lead in the arena, and he knows very well which direction he is travelling and that a corner will be coming up very soon. Much patience and understanding must be afforded to him at this time.

Starting with a half-circle and returning to the track

Canter on the track in normal canter, say, on the right rein starting at 'B'. Ride around the corner 'F' to roughly 'A', making an arc of about 10 or 15 metres, and then canter back to the track on a diagonal line., thus completing a teardrop turn (see Chapter 17). On reaching the track, try to stay in right lead canter on the track for two or three strides before returning to trot (see Figure 16.2).

Don't try to negotiate the corner in counter-counter yet. Make doubly sure that you keep your body in right canter position. The number of

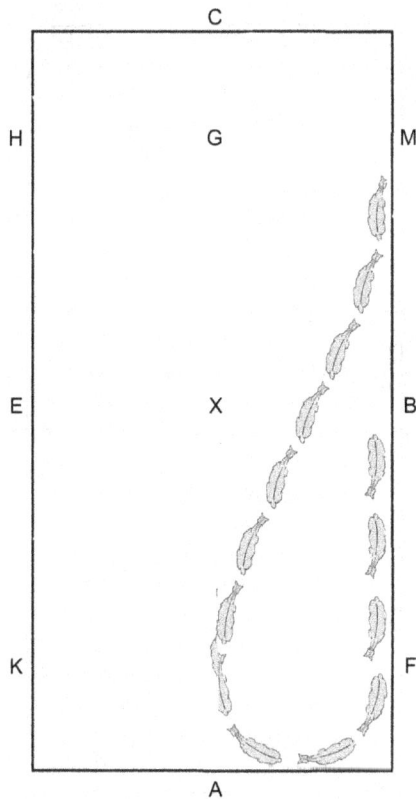

Figure 16.2 The Counter-Canter on a Teardrop Turn
This shows one way of training the counter-canter, utilising the teardrop turn (or demi-volte; see also the diagram of a normal teardrop turn in Chapter 17). Figure courtesy of Lesley Skipper.

counter-canter strides can be gradually built up over time. How much time it takes does not matter as long as the horse remains calm and collected.

When first attempting the corner, make sure you take the corner very wide – don't ride deep into it.

Shallow loops

Shallow loops are often used to train counter-counter. You ride, say, on the left rein, a left lead canter round the corner after 'A', make a shallow loop in towards the centre of the school after 'F', then return to the track at roughly 'B'. The idea is that as you make the loop back to the track, the horse is cantering on the left lead but moving in a right-hand direction (see Figure 16.3).

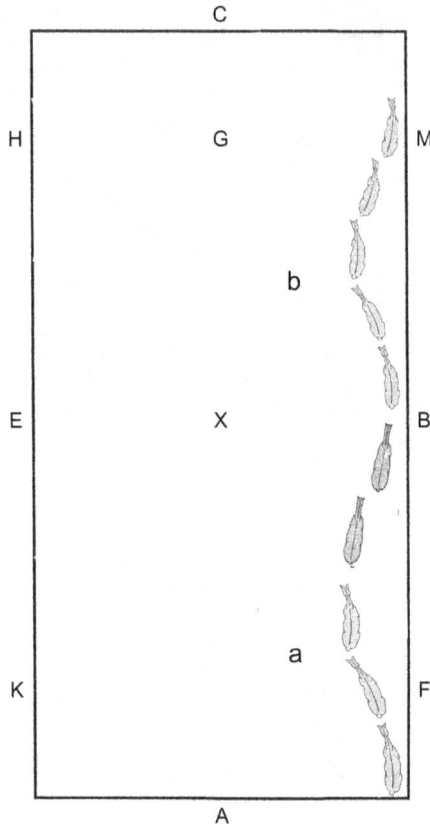

Figure 16.3 Shallow Loops

Utilising shallow loops to train the counter-canter. Figure courtesy of Lesley Skipper.

a) shows normal canter back to track,

b) shows counter-canter back to track.

Personally, I am not a fan of this way of training counter-canter as it often results in a type of canter leg-yield back to the track. It takes a very accomplished rider to keep the horse's body at the correct angle to the track. What usually happens is that the forehand drifts towards the track, and the counter-canter is lost, becoming more like a leg-yield or a straight canter to the track.

Uses of counter-canter

Understanding

A good understanding of the counter-canter can help both horse and rider to consolidate the true canter.

Strengthening

It is used as a strengthening exercise, particularly for the loin and quarter muscles of the horse. Notwithstanding the fact that collection is required before teaching the counter-canter, it should improve the collection.

Straightening

Perhaps the most important use of the counter-canter is to straighten the horse. If a horse swings his quarters inwards at the canter, much use is made of the arena track and wall, which stops the quarters from swinging that way in counter-canter.

Counter-canter is normally taught before the flying change. This is mainly to deter the horse from changing the lead at the corner of the school, and it is clear why the horse should do this as in his mind it must be the correct thing to do.

Having said this, nothing is set in stone, and what suits one horse may not suit another. Some horses may find flying change infinitely easier to understand and perform than counter-canter. If they learn flying change first, providing the aids are very clear and precise, they may find the counter-canter easier to perform later.

The flying change

The flying change is when the horse, in canter, changes the sequence of his legs whilst in the air (the moment of suspension), and on reaching the ground, he is cantering with the opposite leading leg.

Many horses do this naturally whilst at liberty, when changing direction, or to rebalance themselves if they're on the wrong lead when negotiating a bend.

However, I cannot emphasise enough how different it is when under saddle with the added weight of the rider.

Whilst some horses find it fairly easy to perform under saddle, once they are balanced and collected, others do not.

Some experienced horses do it themselves whilst under saddle, when show jumping or riding cross country, without even a request from the rider.

Here is what Paul Belasik says on the subject, in his book *Dressage for the 21st Century* (Ref: 16.3):

> No other movement (flying change) seems to be such a matter of genetics. Horses born with the ability to change can do so correctly from

the first day they are introduced to the movement. Other horses have no inclination to change and training them to do the flying changes can be a long and arduous process.

Even though it is a perfectly natural movement, and young horses will change legs easily at the moment of suspension in canter and gallop when free, many horses struggle with it under the weight of the rider and the constraints of the arena. It is a very advanced movement, and training it too young, or too soon, can be quite damaging. I strongly disapprove of teaching young horses to perform the flying change, even if they have a propensity towards it. It should be left well alone until quite a late stage in the horse's education.

Unfortunately, because it can be a flamboyant, impressive movement, there is a huge tendency for people to teach it too soon.

It is not something, like shoulder-in, where you can start off gently in walk. You either aim for it or you don't.

If your horse is ready for flying change, that is, he is well muscled, balanced and calm and can canter in a reasonably slow, collected canter, then you could begin to request the change.

I think the best place to try this at first is across the diagonal at the centre line. You should canter round the school, coming off the track at the quarter marker, and make your way across the diagonal line. Before reaching the invisible marker 'X' in the middle of the school, ask for a transition back to trot. Trot for a couple of strides, then change the flexion and your body aids, and request a canter strike off on the opposite lead. This is called the simple change and is a preparation for the flying change.

These trot strides can be gradually reduced, over time of course, until you reach the stage of a flying change. If this does not happen fairly easily, you can try coming back to walk and do the same thing in walk; gradually reducing the walk strides until you reach the change. (See walk/canter transitions in Chapter 15.)

Obviously, your aids have to be exact. You need to gently change the flexion of the horse and at the same time reverse your canter aids, for instance, if you're cantering right, and you're going to change to the left, your left hip must come forward and right leg and hip back. Your shoulder position should slightly change, and you must look into the new direction.

All these aids must be done smoothly and without fuss and should be miniscule to the onlooker. The main aid is that of the seat and weight. As you advance the new leading hip, you should automatically be putting a little more weight into the new inside leg (inside of the new bend). This should also automatically slightly lighten your outside hip. This is important

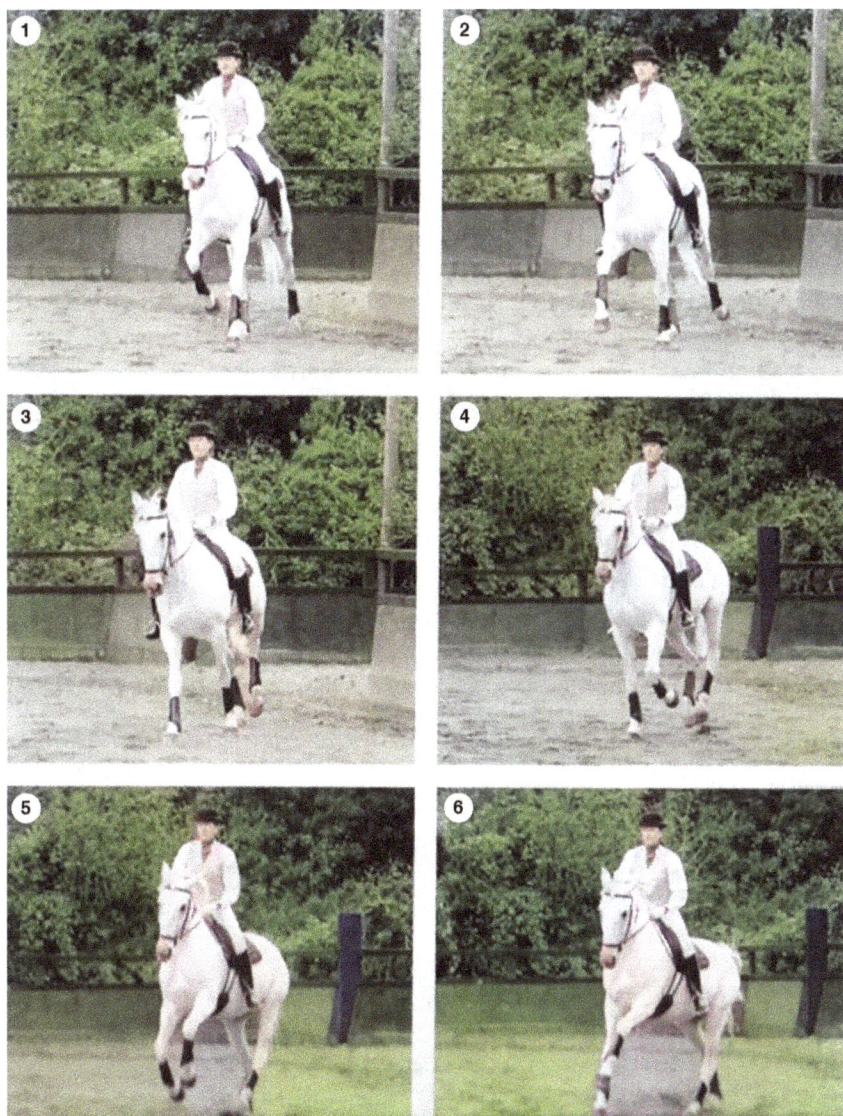

Figure 16.4 Flying Change at Each Stride (Tempi-Changes)

Sylvia Loch on her Lusitano stallion Prazer. These photos and caption are reproduced by kind permission of Sylvia Loch and Kenilworth Press from the book *The Balanced Horse, The Aids by Feel, Not Force*, written by Sylvia Loch and published by and copyright of Kenilworth Press.

'Keeping ourselves and the horse straight and level is the biggest challenge as we prepare for the first change of leg. In Photos 1, 2, and 3, my (right) inside leg can just be seen at the girth supporting the right lead and my weight clearly into the right stirrup. The moment of suspension occurs somewhere between photos 4 and 5, where my left leg moves forward and the unseen leg requests a change of lead (from the right hind). Photo 6 shows left canter and weight into the left stirrup – although in a moment everything will reverse for the next change of leg' (Ref: 16.1). Photos by Nathalie Todd.

as it will allow the horse's new outside hind to come through to initiate the change.

It is common to see riders overdoing these aids and launching themselves from one side of the horse to the other. This is not only ugly but also not helpful and can really unbalance the horse. The aids should be as gentle as possible. If in doubt, do less. It's better to do less and not achieve the goal than to overdo the aids and possibly upset or unbalance the horse.

It is of great advantage if the rider's change of aids can be given either at the moment of suspension, or just as he is about to reach that stage. As mentioned before, the change happens when he is in suspension, and he should change with his hind legs first, then the front legs.

Don't ask for too much bend as it would then be impossible for the horse to change; it's better to straighten him first, and then change the flexion.

Once you have achieved the flying change in the middle of the school, it can obviously be used in other places of the arena, but I would not request it at a corner of the school as this may become a habit, and he may perform the change when counter-cantering.

I will not delve into multiple changes in this book as they are even more advanced and should not be attempted until a much later time in the horse's education.

References

Ref: 16.1 – 'The Balanced Horse – The Aids by Feel, Not Force' – Loch, Sylvia – Kenilworth Press – 2013.

Ref: 16.2 – 'Masters of Equitation on Counter-Canter and Flying Changes' – Compiled by Martin Diggle – J.A. Allen – 2002.

Ref: 16.3 – 'Dressage for the 21st Century' – Belasik, Paul – J.A. Allen – 2001.

Intertwining the exercises

17

Including voltes and demi-voltes

When we have successfully introduced and confirmed all the lateral exercises previously covered in this book, it is time to incorporate and intertwine them within our normal training programme. This is a challenging and exciting time for both horse and rider. We now have a veritable armoury of movements to use in short bursts between our normal two-track riding, thus making boredom or repetition virtually impossible.

Even before reaching this advanced stage with so many exercises at our disposal, I find it extremely annoying when people say 'my horse doesn't like schooling; he finds it boring'. What they really mean is that they have no idea of the proper way to school a horse. Even in the early stages of training, there are so many variations of movements and different ways of intertwining them that boredom is impossible if you have any imagination and know what you are aiming for. But now, at this stage, it is a matter of what to leave out rather than what exercises to practise on a given day.

Trotting round in endless circles, or cantering many circuits of the school, hoping to improve the gait, of course is going to become not only boring but tiring and unnecessarily wearing. As I have said before, it is generally the transitions which improve the gait, not continuing in a gait which is often going further and further downhill.

Never neglect the walk, trot, canter and transitions between the lateral work as these are important for the forward impulsion of the horse (note: forward impulsion as in energy, not speed), but never overdo anything.

DOI: 10.1201/9781003503422-18

Re-assessing and confirming your classical seat

Take plenty of breaks; allow the horse to stretch in walk on a long rein and re-assess your own position. Although you can relax during this time, don't slouch; sit upright, and think about the classical seat. Keep your torso upright with expanded chest; lift your shoulders up and back, and relax them down in order to release any tension which may have built up. Think about whether you have equal weight on each seat-bone with a little weight on your crutch area, including the inner thighs. Relax your legs down with your heel underneath your hip, but keep your legs gently draped around the horse and encourage him, if necessary, to step actively through with his hind legs, even in this period of relative relaxation. You can also use this time to prepare your thoughts for what exercises you think would benefit your horse on that particular day and in which order you are going to practise them.

It is a mistake to concentrate all the time on lateral work, but a few steps in each session, even when you have decided to work on something else, is very beneficial to the horse.

Basic exercises to intertwine

Even in the early stages of training, when most of the exercises are beyond you and your horse, you can still intertwine and change so many of the basic ones to make schooling varied and interesting.

For instance, you could ride a 20-metre circle at 'A', say in walk on the left rein, and then, on completing the circle back at 'A', break into trot until you reach 'H', change the rein 'H' to 'F', go back to walk and ride a 20-metre walk circle on the right rein at 'A'. You could then ride a serpentine in walk; then do the same circle exercise at the 'C' end of the arena. You could also incorporate a 20-metre circle in the centre of the school. In this way, you will be making plenty of changes of rein and walk to trot transitions, and the horse will be eager to know what is coming next. Plus, you're not riding endless circles.

Serpentines also can be ridden in walk, even in the early stages of training.

Don't forget to take plenty of breaks, allowing the horse to walk on a long rein.

Suggestions of more advanced exercises to intertwine

Sequence of exercises starting on left rein from 'A':

Shoulder-in between 'F' and 'B'.
Travers between 'B' and 'M'.

Figure 17.1 Good Collection

Rita Ling on her Lusitano Stallion, Barao. Photo by John Ling.

At 'M', Quarters back to track.

Proceed on track, and turn left down centre line at 'C'.

From centre line at 'C', leg-yield to the right, reaching track around 'E'.

Ride on round track to 'A'.

Turn left down centre line at 'A', and half-pass to the left back to track at 'E'.

You have now changed the rein to the right, and I suggest you take a break. To ride the same exercise in the other direction, follow these steps:

At 'E', change to right flexion on track to 'M'.

Shoulder-in from 'M' to 'B'.

Travers from 'B' to 'F'.

Quarters back to track, and proceed to 'A'.

Turn down centre line at 'A'.

Left leg-yield towards 'E'.

Ride on round track to 'C'.

From centre line at 'C', turn right and half-pass to the right back to 'E'.

You are now back on the left rein, from whence you started, having completed the same procedure on both reins.

In these sequences, the travers can sometimes be substituted by the renvers, but of course, this is much more difficult, and you will need to bring the forehand back to the track and change the bend before reaching the corner.

Exercises incorporating canter work in between lateral steps

Starting on, say, the left rein at 'A' in trot, ride shoulder-in from 'F' to 'B'. At 'B' strike off into a left canter in a semi-circle across the arena until you reach roughly 'E' on the opposite track; then return to trot. Ride in trot round the track until you reach 'A', and return to walk. Now you can either take a break (which I would suggest if your horse is new to this work), or change the rein using a demi-pirouette (turn on the haunches). Then go back to trot, and ride the same sequence on the other rein; congratulate the horse, and take a break. This is an extremely exacting and quite strenuous exercise and should not be attempted until the horse is easily able to take weight on his haunches and preferably has already mastered canter to walk. Even though you are not asking him to walk from the canter in this sequence, it will help if he is capable of it. He will have to have a good deal of collection for any of this to be possible.

You don't have to be exactly accurate with regard to reaching the required dressage letter, but it will help as a guide, and you can aim for accuracy later on.

The shoulder-in prior to the canter should greatly enhance the collection in the canter strike off.

At first, you may need to straighten the horse out of the shoulder-in before the strike off, but as time goes on, he will cope with this change of movement very quickly.

Another variation to this exercise, which in some ways is even more exacting, is as follows: after riding your trot shoulder-in, then your canter semi-circle, return to trot shoulder-in at the halfway marker rather than continuing in a two-track normal trot. In other words, you are going directly from canter into a trot shoulder-in. Many horses find this quite surprising, but when they are correctly and slowly prepared, it is enthralling for both horse and rider. It is very demanding of the rider as well as the horse as you have to be spot-on and quick with the change of aids but, at the same time, subtle and gentle.

Just because your horse can perhaps perform a good trot shoulder-in halfway down the long side of the school does not necessarily mean he will be able to strike off into canter immediately, and he will find it even more difficult to come immediately from canter back to trot shoulder-in. So, *be patient* – never pull on the mouth or use any sort of force. If you miss the marker, it doesn't matter that much; what matters is a smooth transition if at all possible. Always look at your own position and aiding, which needs to be exemplary for this type of work. The horse will need all the help you can give with your body posture and correct use of aids.

Exercises on the circle

Moving in and out on the circle or 'spiralling'

The first and easiest lateral exercise on the circle is the leg-yield, where you gradually decrease the circle, putting more weight into your inside stirrup/seat-bone, requesting the horse to step to the inside. Your outside leg applied slightly behind the girth can gently request the movement to the inside. Your outside hand should gently but firmly support the horse on the outside, confirming the request to move sideways to the inside of the circle. Your inside hand confirms the inside flexion with gentle give and take or squeezing actions as and when necessary. Your inside leg is held supportively at the girth, underneath your inside hip, which should be advanced.

When you have reached the required smaller circle, you then ask for a leg-yield gradually outwards. Return some weight to the outside stirrup/seat-bone, keeping your legs and hips in the same position but changing the emphasis by gently pushing or nudging with your inside leg. Your outside leg prevents the quarters from swinging out. Your outside hand still supports the horse's outside shoulder but allows the horse to move to the outside.

There are many more advanced lateral exercises which can be used on the circle. They are generally much more difficult when performed there because of the lack of support and point of reference, which is offered by the wall of the arena. However, correct performance on the circle is certain confirmation of the horse's understanding, agility and obedience and requires good, tactful, precise yet gentle aiding from the rider.

It is best to begin in walk. Try riding half a circle in shoulder-in, then another half in travers.

Shoulder-out can be incorporated as well. Shoulder-out is merely shoulder-in ridden in a different place, but it can be quite difficult on the circle. You could ride shoulder-out for, say, a quarter of the circle, change to shoulder-in for another quarter and then ride travers for the next quarter. Then (if you are really brave), take the quarters back to the line of the circle, take the forehand inwards, change the bend and ride renvers for the remaining quarter circle – then your circle is complete.

Gradually build up the sequences

Gradually build up the sequences of all these exercises by just riding one part at first, say, one trot shoulder-in to canter, then rest. When that becomes easy, continue as described earlier. Obviously, the trot shoulder-in can be substituted by a walk shoulder-in, which requires the horse to strike off directly into canter from the walk shoulder-in. This often improves the quality and collection of the canter immensely, but make sure your horse is ready and strong enough for it and can already perform a canter strike off fairly easily from walk on a straight line.

As you can see, the possible combinations of these exercises are almost endless. As always, when you have practised something on one rein, it should be done on the other.

If your horse is finding one particular movement too difficult, then sub-stitute it for one which he finds easier, and go back to practising the difficult movement on the track, possibly at a later date.

Voltes, demi-voltes and changes of rein

A volte is a small circle, and a demi-volte is half a small circle, usually ridden from the track at the centre marker (either 'A' or 'C') on the short side of the school. This small circle or volte should be no less than a 10-metre circle (although it can be even smaller when the horse is extremely advanced).

To ride a demi-volte, say on the left rein, you would come off the track, say at 'C', ride a semi-circle, or demi-volte, then straighten the horse and head back to the track at around 'B', thereby changing the rein. This is often known as a 'teardrop turn' (see Figure 17.2). These are a useful addition to the movements to add even more variety in-between the other exercises. They are good in that you are bending the horse in the semi-circle, then straightening him to ride back to the track and then changing the flexion on reaching the track in order to have a small amount of bend or flexion, as required when riding straight down the track on the opposite rein. Always practise them on both reins – perhaps not immediately, but maybe after incorporating other exercises.

The demi-volte or teardrop turn is required in some novice dressage tests, but I would say that the full 10-metre circle, or volte, should not be ridden in

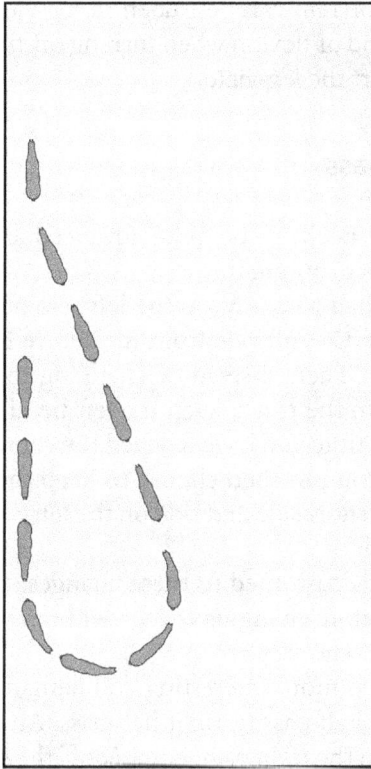

Figure 17.2 Demi-Volte or Teardrop Turn
This figure shows how to make a demi-volte, which is a useful, and more challenging, way to change the rein when intertwining the exercises. Figure courtesy of Lesley Skipper.

anything other than walk until the horse is quite advanced in education and accompanying strength, balance and flexibility.

The teardrop turn, or demi-volte, is one way of changing the rein, but there are plenty of others, such as the following:

Change of rein across the diagonal from one quarter marker to the other –
    e.g., from 'K' to 'M', or 'F' to 'H', or 'H' to 'F', or 'M' to 'K'
Demi-pirouette – in walk or trot as described in Chapter 8
From one halfway marker to the other – e.g., 'E' to 'B' or 'B' to 'E'

You can also change the rein by riding half-pass from the centre marker either at 'C' or 'A', then on reaching the track at around the halfway marker, change the bend in preparation for riding on the opposite rein.

The same change of rein can be ridden in leg-yield, but then you will need to change the bend or flexion when turning off the track at the halfway marker before you start the leg-yield.

Leg-yield to half-pass

Obviously, your horse needs to be quite advanced and well established in half-pass before you incorporate this.

You can try riding half-pass, say, on the left rein after the corner at 'M'. Come off the track at 'C', and ride from the centre line back to the track, aiming for around 'B'. Then, instead of changing the bend and riding on the opposite rein down the track, keep the left bend and leg-yield back to the centre line. By the time you have reached the centre line, you should be somewhere near 'A'. You can then choose to keep the left bend when you reach the track on the short side and ride on the left rein, or you can change the bend and turn right.

When the horse is accustomed to these changes, the number of strides you ride in half-pass before changing to leg-yield can be reduced, so you are zig-zagging across the school.

To make things even more interesting and demanding, you can zig-zag by changing from left half-pass to right half-pass. An example would be to ride in half-pass, say on the right rein, coming off the short side of the track at 'C', and then ride in half-pass back to the track, aiming roughly for 'E'. Then change the bend, and ride in half-pass back to the track towards the centre line. The number of strides can be reduced eventually, but this will be extremely exacting and quite strenuous.

You will need to straighten the horse momentarily when changing from one half-pass to the other. Obviously, since the forehand is in advance of the quarters in this exercise, you will have to re-align the quarters to the forehand before changing the bend and asking for the forehand to again precede the quarters in the new direction and bend. This may take a little while to perfect, but as you both become au fait with these movements, the change of bend and direction will become smoother.

The number of combinations of all these exercises is almost limitless, and you could never fit them all into one schooling session, so don't try; it would be too exhausting and mind blowing!

Time and patience are what is needed most of all

Most of the exercises described here are advanced ones, and to be able to perform them in quick succession in the way described takes years of preparation, so don't be put off at how difficult it seems when you first begin.

Conclusion

One thing's for sure – you and your horse will never, ever be bored, and you should both enjoy the challenge presented to you. Don't try to do too much too soon; keep something in hand to practise the next day. Enjoy every little bit of improvement, and view each setback (and there will be some) as a learning opportunity. Think about why it went wrong – is the horse ready for this? – were my aids/body position/weight aids correct? Always be pleased with your horse for trying, and he will enjoy the work as much as you should.

Figure 17.3 Relaxing

My position is not the best in this shot, but both Secret and I are completely happy and relaxed, in unity with one another, after a good and exhilarating schooling session. Photo by Kathleen Goulden.

My hope is that this book will help readers to achieve unity between horse and rider. When you have a close relationship with a horse, based on love and respect on both sides, then you have something more wonderful than money or fame. It lifts the spirit beyond anything any non-horse person could imagine.

It does not mean allowing your horse to do just as he pleases, but you should be a reliable leader and protector. In turn, your horse will not only willingly co-operate but also enjoy the process and have a desire to protect you as much as he can.

I would go as far as to say that for any horse person, classical riding is the key to a happy life for horse and human alike.

Index

Note: Page numbers in *italics* indicate a figure on the corresponding page.

For Product Safety Concerns and Information please contact our EU
representative GPSR@taylorandfrancis.com
Taylor & Francis Verlag GmbH, Kaufingerstraße 24, 80331 München, Germany

9 781032 790817